FINANCIAL SECURITY FOR WOMEN

•

*Using Your
Head AND Heart
to Achieve It*

By Mary F. Ivins, CFP

SYMMETRY PUBLISHING COMPANY

Chicago, Illinois

Financial Security for Women:
Using Your Head AND Heart to Achieve It
By Mary F. Ivins, CFP

Published by Symmetry Publishing Company
P. O. Box 81950, Chicago, Illinois 60681-0950
E-mail symetrypub@aol.com

Cover design by Patrick Carr
Editing by Robin Quinn
Interior layout by Sue Knopf

Corporations and Schools: Financial Security for Women is available at quantity discount with a bulk purchase for education, business or sales promotional use. For further information, please contact Symmetry Publishing Company, P. O. Box 81950, Chicago, Illinois 60681-0950.

Library of Congress Catalog Card Number: 99-90773

Printed in the United States of America
First Printing November 1999

Publishers Cataloging-in-Publication
(Provided by Quality Books, Inc.)

Ivins, Mary F.
      Financial security for women : using your head and heart to achieve it / by Mary F. Ivins. -- 1st ed.
      p. cm.
      Includes bibliographical references and index.
      LCCN: 99-90773
      ISBN: 0-9671095-0-7

      1. Women--Finance, Personal. 2. Financial security. 3. Finance, Personal--Psychological aspects. I. Title.

HG179.I85 1999   332.024'042
            QBI99-1060

*"In the midst of winter, I finally learned
that there was in me an invincible summer."*

ALBERT CAMUS, French novelist, essayist & playwright

$$\Sigma$$

The above Greek symbol signifies "the sum of the total."
We are our experiences.
I give thanks for
all circumstances that have helped to
shape my destiny. This includes each
individual, including those with whom I
have had a personal relationship—
particularly my mother and father and those
who always believed in me—as well as
those who failed to support me. I especially
give thanks for those who have influenced
my Becoming through their
writings.

CREDITS

I would like to gratefully thank the following authors, their agents, and publishers and other financial service companies for granting permission to include excerpts from the following:

- Christopher Hayes, Ph.D., and Kate Kelly, Doubleday, New York, NY, *Money Makeovers*

- Al Siebert, Ph.D., *The Survivor Personality*

- Michael Le Boeuf, Ph.D., The Pine Agency, New York, NY, *Working Smart*

- Beyond Words Publishing Company, Inc., "Corporate Mission Statement"

- Joel H. Weldon & Associates, Inc., "Success Comes in Cans—Not in Cannots"

- Irene Tanner, Suited for Success

- OppenheimerFunds, Inc., Statistics and Research

- Portfolio Management Consultants (PMC) Statistical Information for Graphs

- Steve Yakush, Executive Director of Master Mind Publishing, *Master Mind Goal Achiever's Journal 1999*

- Newkirk Products, Inc., Estimated Retirement Income Worksheet

ACKNOWLEDGMENTS

As with all worthwhile endeavors, many individuals were involved with making this book happen. Accordingly, I would like to thank the following people. Unfortunately some of them may question how they could be included on this list since appearances were that they did not support my project. However I sincerely believe that obstacles are placed in our path to make us strive harder. This then is a book that these individuals helped to create:

The editor, Robin Quinn, Word for Word, Los Angeles, California, did what her slogan says: "Together We'll Make Your Ideas Sparkle!"

The graphic designer, Sue Knopf, Graffolio, La Crosse, Wisconsin, lived up to her reputation as "amazing."

Company logo, book-cover designer, Patrick Carr, Photography and Graphics, Chicago, Illinois.

Indexer, Tina M. Trettin, Chicago, Illinois.

Gold foil die manufacturer, Paul Murphy, E. C. Schultz and Company, Elk Grove Village, Illinois.

Literary Agents, Editors, etc:

Elizabeth Lyons, author of *Non-Fiction Book Proposals,* Hillsboro, Oregon; Sonia Nordenson, Editor, Ojai, California; Natasha Kern, Literary Agent, Natasha Kern Agency, Portland, Oregon; and Connie Goddard, Literary Agent, Goddard Book Group, Chicago, Illinois.

Outstanding Support People:

Scott Wilkinson, Portfolio Management Consultants (PMC), Denver, Colorado; Vicky Hill, friend and ex-neighbor, Chicago, Illinois; Barbara Shaffer, friend, Chicago, Illinois; and Mary Bernice Lamb, mentor, Effingham, Illinois.

Other Individuals Who Have Shared My Path:

Paul J. Wagner, first husband; Walter Najacht, second husband; Richard A. Karhuse, significant other for 12 years; Michael P., John J., Robert L. and William S. Wagner, sons. Paula Wagner Walser and Mary Elizabeth Wagner Petrisin, daughters. Roberta Ivins Rigali and Dr. Judith Ivins Aschermann, sisters; and Lawrence E. Ivins, brother. Mary and John Murphy, maternal grandparents; Gladys Murphy, aunt by marriage; Mary and Robert Ivins, aunt and uncle. Elizabeth Wagner, former mother-in-law—now deceased; Nicholas Logothetis, business advisor; Tom Lanahan, General Agent for a large insurance company; and Steven Wescott, co-worker.

In addition, throughout the book, I have included kudos to individuals who appeared in my life in order that I might grow: Linda Dobey, Trend Designs; Hermy Stone; Irene Tanner, Suited for Success; Gwen Gillespie, Science of the Mind Church; Richard Karhuse, Lucent Technologies; Mary Jane Barrett Butler; Kay Cahan; Rev. Michael C. Rann, Science of the Mind Church; Janice Heller, CPA; and Mikel Cirkus, friend and graphic designer.

CONTENTS

WARNING—DISCLAIMER

The sole purpose of this book is to give inspiration and information with regard to becoming financially independent. The book is not rendering legal, accounting or other professional advice. Therefore, the author and publisher will not accept responsibility for offering advice that is not within the author's jurisdiction. A competent professional should be sought if there is a need for professional counseling.

This book is not intended to be the ultimate source; rather it is to be used in conjunction with other resources. To take advantage of this powerful learning opportunity, you are encouraged to visit and experience some or all of the books and resources contained in the Appendix.

Learning how to be financially independent is not a quick process; it, like most things that are worthwhile, will take time. However, the effort is worth it in peace of mind and self-fulfillment.

We have endeavored to offer correct information; however, at times well-meant and sincere efforts go astray. If there are mistakes in this book, please let the author/publisher know and they will be corrected in subsequent editions. Remember, this book is offered as a general guide and not as an ultimate source. The information is timely, and although the stock and bond markets are moving targets, focusing on the long-term gives success.

As stated in the preface, the purpose of this book is to inspire and teach. The author and Symmetry Publishing shall have neither liability nor responsibility to any person or entity for loss or damage caused or alleged to have been caused by information contained in this book.

If you do not desire to be bound by the above disclaimer, please return the book immediately. It is our policy to give a full refund to anyone who feels that the book is not suitable for her/his needs.

PART

I

Getting Started

Preface

Women, Self-Confidence, & Financial Security

". . . taking charge of one's money has been the 'last frontier' for women. Though women have made progress in the workforce and can now be found on almost every rung of the corporate ladder, they often leave their own financial situation on the back burner."

CHRISTOPHER HAYES, PH.D., *Money Makeovers*

During my more than 15 years as an advisor on wealth accumulation, I have noticed that many women lack the necessary self-confidence to take control of their financial future. At first I didn't understand their reluctance and had the attitude, "If I can do it, why can't you?" I was guilty of forgetting where I came from.

Then I encountered the work of Christopher Hayes, Ph.D., founder of the National Center for Women and Retirement Research and author of the book, *Money Makeovers*. Hayes reports that the lack of skill and interest in investing on the part of many women has more to do with self-perceptions about their own abilities than their actual abilities. And he believes this is the result of their early education and family experiences.

So if you are a woman who finds it difficult to take control of your financial future, you are not alone. According to a study conducted by OppenheimerFunds, Inc. (one of the largest and oldest firms offering mutual funds), less than 12% of women, living and planning with a partner, make their own investment decisions. To more fully under-

3

stand the "why" behind this statistic, we must look again at women's self-perceptions and the reasons people act the way they do.

In his book, *The Survivor Personality,* Al Siebert, Ph.D., writes that the majority of our behavior is dictated by what we think others think of us. Few of us are self-directed. And a landmark study, the Hawthorne Effect, partially conducted by Rosenthal & Jacobsen, 1968, empirically proved Siebert's observations. In the study, these researchers arbitrarily divided a set of school children into two groups. The teacher of one of these groups was told that all of the children in her section were "exceptional" and that they would out-perform the other class, which was said to be made up of "average" achievers. What happened was exactly as predicted. The group of students whose teacher believed in them actually became exceptional children who DID perform astonishingly better than the other section of children.

Because so many women believe that the world of investments is an arena where they will not excel, they lack the necessary self-confidence to step forward and take control of their financial future. I have created this book, *Financial Security for Women,* in an effort to inspire female readers to take risks and to learn about successful investing. Furthermore, I go on record as stating that I believe in your desire and commitment to use the wonderful creative power that is within each of us to make a huge, beneficial difference in your own individual life, and to then expand this to all of humankind. YOU CAN DO IT!

Change will require that you take the necessary action, and my book will assist you in both preparing to take action and in actually doing so. In Part I, *Getting Started,* you are learning where women stand today in terms of investing, and what I will be covering in this book. In Part II, *Removing the Psychological Blocks to Financial Independence,* you will discover how to make important adjustments in your attitudes and beliefs related to your investment abilities. And in Part III, *Unleashing Your Analytical Ability & Owning the Success Formula,* you will master the technical background necessary for savvy investing. The problem-solving and analytical abilities to achieve financial freedom are lying dormant in women, says Hayes. It is my goal to awaken and strengthen that part of you.

Hayes further states that women need role models to reinforce their belief that they have the power to do and become whatever they desire. Humbly I submit myself as your role model. At age 49, after spending my entire adult life as a homemaker, I had to master the necessary emotional growth and technical knowledge to become financially independent. It is my wish that reviewing my life experiences will empower you.

As I am certain that there are many unreported stories of women's success—"rags to riches" tales of achievement accomplished through an individual's own efforts—I would like you to help me discover them. Write to me and provide these women's names, addresses and telephone numbers. I will send these achievers an information-gathering form and interview them for a follow-up book. "His" story (history) has been told, "hers" has not. Together we can change this.

By combining newly acquired analytical skills with your inherent coping ability, you will create your ideal life. Sarah Ban Breathnach in her wonderful book, *Simple Abundance,* points out that most women have learned through necessity to cope. She says, ". . . if women who cope well ran everything, Nirvana wouldn't only be the name of a grunge band." We can create this Nirvana. After reading my book, you will know what you must do.

Mary F. Ivins, CFP
Chicago, Illinois
October 1999

The Head & Heart Approach to Investing

"To achieve success in all areas of our lives, we must learn to integrate the head and the heart, the scientific and the spiritual, the practical and the intuitive, the Western technology and the Eastern philosophy."

MARY F. IVINS, CFP

Do you want to get rid of that "wolf at my heels" feeling, to experience more peace in your days and in your environment, to enjoy life more and get what you want out of it, and to have all of the money that you'll require in the years ahead? This book will tell you how, but you'll need to do the work. There is a Zen proverb that says, "When the student is ready, the teacher will appear." Are you ready? If so, this book will help you turn your "readiness" into "willingness" so you can manifest unimaginable good in your life.

According to Hayes, 75% of women place their money in low-yield-type accounts, such as Certificates of Deposit (CDs), money markets, savings plans or government issues of Treasury bills, notes and bonds. Although many women are expected to bring home a paycheck and often handle the checkbook and pay the bills, gender bias still exists; investment decisions usually are left to the male gender. Well, the time has come to change these statistics and patterns.

In fact, not only has the time come, such change is mandatory or women will have many regrets. After 10 years of research involving thousands of women, Hayes concludes that "Between one-third and two-thirds of women now aged thirty-five to fifty-five will be impoverished after age sixty-five if they do not immediately start to prepare financially for their later years." And he notes that many of them will be "shocked by their predicament." By reading *Financial Security for Women,* you are opening up your awareness, and can thus avoid such a rude surprise in your later life.

Why I Wrote This Book

As more and more women become aware of their potential financial vulnerability regarding their senior years, they naturally begin to question why they have not taken this important aspect of their lives more seriously. A few books have emerged in an attempt to answer this question. Though some explore the psychological blocks women have related to investing, I feel these books have not gone into this issue in enough depth. And I've noticed that the books tend to concentrate on reviewing the past to help a woman understand her current behavior.

As I first considered writing *Financial Security for Women,* I saw the need to create a book that would focus on the pivotal "Now Moments" rather than stress hang-ups from the reader's past. I decided that I would deliver the metaphysical principles—the obscure and less obvious answers—that would enable a woman to change her present way of thinking and feelings about herself and investing.

When I mention the term "metaphysical," I am referring to moving the reader into a spiritual realm. The term "metaphysical" literally means "beyond the physical." By applying metaphysical/spiritual principles to your life, you will discover that you are stronger and more capable than you have ever realized.

Taking a new approach to investment counseling, my book, *Financial Security for Women: Using Your Head AND Heart to Achieve It,* will combine metaphysical/spiritual principles with practical investment advice and theory in an in-depth manner. Reading this material will enable a woman to confront her psychological blocks, change her attitude, and move forward to acquire the technical background she'll need to become a savvy investor. After tackling her inner blocks, a woman's heart will be on her side as she explores the investment world. Then she can go on to use her head to evaluate the choices before her.

What You'll Learn about Investing

Traditionally women have been taught to seek security, so it can be difficult for them to make financial decisions that involve real or perceived risk. And because they may shun things technical, it can be hard for women to determine what the degree of risk truly is. Spreadsheets often don't speak to them.

However, to become financially successful, women must use their analytical (cognitive) reasoning as well as their intuition. In fact, many believe that it is from the "known" (the technical) that we learn about the "unknown" (intuition). Both intuition and reasoning will play important roles in your future investment decisions.

So on the practical side, the technical advice in *Financial Security for Women* will show you how to:

- Develop realistic expectations regarding investment results,

- Understand how economic forces affect the investment returns on different asset classes,

- Obtain knowledge on historical rates of return for different asset classes—both in long- and short-term periods,

- Take some investment risk for long-term goals,

- Understand risk/reward tradeoffs,

- Review hypothetical investment returns of various portfolios based on historical data,

- Successfully employ various methods of investing,

- Create a portfolio of mutual funds, and

- Structure a stock and bond portfolio.

As you can see, there is much to be learned from this book. My recommendation for your first reading is that you skim through the book and slow down in certain sections to absorb the knowledge you need right away. Later you can revisit the book time and time again, and with each reading, you will increasingly grasp more and more of the technical aspects of investing.

My Story

My life experiences are sprinkled throughout *Financial Security for Women* in order to show you the path I took to becoming financially savvy and secure. It wasn't easy. At age 49, I was divorced for the second time after having been married all of my adult life. I needed to learn to manage financial assets if I were to survive. Necessity overcame my fear.

At age 50, I attained my stockbroker's license; at 53, my Certified Financial Planner designation. At 55, I was accepted into the Registry for Financial Planning Practitioners; and at 60, I established my own firm—I*vins Financial Associates*—and also achieved Registered Investment Advisor status. Now, at age 66, I am on course to attain my dream of becoming a millionaire by 2002.

Of course, having sufficient money is important, but I also believe that true success is measured in our joy of living. Have you noticed that your joy increases as you see yourself getting somewhere? It is this author's hope that my financial successes and "joie de vivre" will inspire you to higher achievement.

What's Ahead

Since women tend to have their own unique blocks towards truly taking charge of their financial future, many must first work at changing their thinking and feelings before developing those new skills. I have laid out the book with this in mind. Thus Part I, *Getting Started,* provides an overview of the book as well as the current situation women are facing regarding investing. Part II, *Removing the Psychological Blocks to Financial Independence,* addresses powerful metaphysical principles that will help women grow out of old, self-defeating behaviors. And Part III, *Unleashing Your Analytical Ability & Owning the Success Formula,* will cover the technical financial information. As we are now near the end of Part I, let's take a closer look at what will be covered in the other two sections.

Part II will deal with the heart part of this book's title: *Financial Security for Women: Using Your Head AND Heart to Achieve It.* This section will assist women in working through their early social conditioning.

Part II, "Removing the Psychological Blocks to Financial Independence," will explore:

- Believing in Yourself,

- Having an "I Can" Attitude,

- Adopting Winning Personality Traits,

- Developing a "Money Consciousness," and

- Setting Realistic Goals for Self-Improvement.

After addressing the psychological and spiritual aspects of investing in Part II, we'll move on to Part III where you'll learn how to use your *head* to make and keep money. We will look at the major reasons people fail financially as well as introduce a unique system of investing that I developed called "The Success Formula for Financial Independence."

A note on the Success Formula: Like the elements in any formula, each variable within the Success Formula affects the others that are included. It will not be enough for you to just familiarize yourself with the formula. In order to achieve financial success, you will need to "own" the formula, learning to skillfully employ each variable.

And so Part III, "Unleashing Your Analytical Ability & Owning the Success Formula," will deal with:

- Examining Reasons Why People Fail Financially,

- Recognizing the Time Value of Money,

- Pursuing Perfect Health,

- Integrating Inflation Protection,

- Creating a Tax-Favored Environment,

- Understanding Return on Investment (ROI),

- Grasping the Risk/Reward Pyramid, and

- Structuring Mutual Fund and Stock and Bond Portfolios.

Following the final chapter of the book, which salutes you for getting that far and supports you in your decision to make a new beginning, you'll find the Glossary, Resources, Bibliography and Index. Note that the books in the Bibliography fall into two categories: philosophy and investing. My advice is to seek out those books that "speak" to you with a blend of books from both sides. And don't worry about the date the book was published. Investment principles and the philosophy of life have not changed. Also, the Glossary is quite extensive, and can be helpful to you as you grasp new financial principles.

Thoughts to Accompany You on the Journey

Before we start the journey, I'd like to share several thoughts for you to keep in mind. First, it's important for you to remember that you are not alone. You have a Partner who will be there to help you to create your ideal world. It doesn't matter what you call this Partner—God, Yahweh, the Force, Buddha, Christ, Higher Self, Chi, Prana, etc.—simply unequivocally believe in It. I will refer to this Partner as God at times, and also use some of the other terms. Interpret this in your own way.

Secondly, we must be open to accepting the things that show up in our lives as every thing/person we attract is meant to teach us something. This is what Life is all about—growing and expanding our consciousness. It has taken me most of my life to learn this simple lesson.

Lastly, every author has a message. Mine is encapsulated in the quote that began this chapter: "To achieve success in all areas of our lives, we must learn to integrate the head and the heart, the scientific and the spiritual, the practical and the intuitive, the Western technology and the Eastern philosophy." I know that by working from these two fronts, you will become a better investor—and human being.

With these ideas in mind, let us begin our journey. We are two seekers of the Truth. Let us feel the tugging between what would seem to be two opposite forces—the subjective (spiritual) and objective (worldly)—but know there is really only one Force. Let us flow with this Force in order to soar to a limitless life.

"Every day, try to do something foolish,
something creative, and something generous."

BENJAMIN GRAHAM, famous 1930s value investor

Removing the Psychological Blocks to Financial Independence

CHAPTER

Believing in Yourself

"Whatever the mind of man can conceive and believe,
it can achieve."

NAPOLEON HILL, *Think and Grow Rich*

U nlike many other books on investing, which deal solely with the
how to's of committing money for a return, *Financial Security
for Women* includes material to raise your consciousness and boost your
belief in self. No one's opinion of you is more important than your
own. Belief in your ability to make the important decisions that will
impact your life has a substantial influence on how self-directed you
are and how much risk you are willing to take. Therefore I decided to
start the psychological part of this book with a chapter that focuses on
developing the self-confidence required for success with finances and
other aspects of life.

Research by Christopher Hayes, Ph.D., founder of the National
Center for Women and Retirement Research, has shown that women
need to remove psychological blocks in order to become successful
investors. Hayes also feels that women require role models that they
can identify with. Part II of *Financial Security for Women* is an answer
to both those needs. It features hands-on exercises, self-administered
quizzes, and experiences from my own life that have been included to
help the reader move through emotional barriers.

Women & Investing

Before I share the story of how I learned to survive financially on my
own and to invest successfully, let's review some of the available statistics that relate to women and investing. According to recent studies:

- More and more women are living alone: between 1970 and 1994, the number of women living alone doubled from 7 million to 14 million. (Source: US Census Bureau)

- In 1995, women alone who managed families numbered 12.2 million, or 18% of the US population. (Source: US Census Bureau)

- Most single women will have only one-third to one-fifth of the money they'll need to retire comfortably. (Source: OppenheimerFunds, Inc.)

- Approximately 75% of the women who make their own investment choices save in taxable, low-yielding bank-type accounts. (Source: National Center for Retirement Research)

- Women earn approximately 72% of what men earn. (Source: US Census Bureau)

- Historically, almost half of all marriages have ended in divorce. (Source: National Center for Health Statistics)

- Women, on average, outlive their mates by seven years. (Source: National Center for Health Statistics)

- The proportion of women who had never married tripled from 1970 to 1994, from 6% to 20%. (Source: US Census Bureau)

Do you see yourself in one or more of the first six statistics? Are you or will you be represented by any of the last three statistics?

Though the message that these findings brings is not reassuring, it is clear. Women need to drastically change their attitudes and behavior with regard to providing for their security in the years ahead. I do not share these statistics to scare you, but to warn you. By ignoring brutal realities, women can set themselves up for a potential financial disaster. Don't think that you will never be faced with this type of problem. Probabilities are great that you already belong, or will in the future be part of, one or more of the vulnerable groups described above.

You Could Say I've Been There

I speak from experience regarding the potential financial vulnerability of women. Here is my story.

In 1952 at age 19, I entered a marriage that lasted 23 years. During that period, I stayed in the home to raise our six children. My role in that first marriage reflected the times. Recently someone gave me an article that discussed a 1950s home economics textbook. What the article said about the responsibilities of a married woman of that era was identical with the way I patterned my married life.

My husband had descended from a first-generation German family. His mother became my role model. Unlike my family's rather relaxed Irish ways, her household was run with precision. However, no matter how hard I tried, my efforts at being a perfect wife and mother fell short of her and my husband's expectations. Yet based on what most of society believed at the time, I felt that I should be content.

Even though my husband is and was a good person, his upbringing did not prepare him to communicate with our family. Whenever one of the children asked permission for something, he immediately said, "No." This behavior was in keeping with the patriarchal upbringing he had experienced.

Therefore I turned to a male family friend to help me raise my boys. When this friend took a romantic interest in me, I found that I was hungry for the attention that I had not received from my husband. Although this man and I had a romantic relationship for many years, I waited until the oldest child was 22 before asking for a divorce. Being in love, I did not heed the good advice given by my closest woman friend, Hermy, and instead remarried shortly after my first divorce.

Hermy told me that since I had never been on my own in my entire adult life, I should have this experience before entering another marriage. How prophetic she was! I was still the naïve little girl, having very little money of my own even though I was now almost 43.

The reason for my lack of financial resources was that my first husband learned of my other relationship. He threatened to make it all public if I did not accept a very unfair divorce settlement. After 23 years of marriage, having mothered six children, I received an initial $10,000 from the re-mortgaging of the family home. My first husband continued to live in the house for almost five years, subsequently selling it when he remarried and retired at age 52 to Hilton Head, South Carolina. I did not receive my full divorce settlement until almost five years after my first divorce. And after paying capital gains taxes on this second amount, I probably netted around $20,000. This, added to my original $10,000, was what I had to show for 23 years of marriage.

During the first four years of my second marriage, I lived in Effingham, Illinois. I continued being a full-time homemaker while attending Eastern Illinois University part-time. My goal was to become eligible to enter the university's Masters in Business Administration (MBA) program. When we subsequently moved to Indiana, I had 21 credits in the pre-MBA requisite courses. I lacked just one three-credit course in calculus.

While in Illinois, I had worked constantly to improve our home. Again, after moving to Indiana, I worked at painting and fixing up our new house. As will be related later, I received none of the increased equity in either of the homes.

I would have continued living my life in the same old way, however my oldest daughter, Paula, who was then living with us, was adamant that I get a paying job. She is a forward-looking woman and feared for my future. So at age $47\frac{1}{2}$, I ventured into the work world. Not valuing myself very highly, I accepted a commission-only job, earning 25 cents for every dollar I made for the owner of a placement office. After seven months, my second husband and I moved to Little Rock, Arkansas. I took another commission-only position at a search firm. Now I only had to give back 50 cents for each dollar I brought in.

Five months later, at age 49, I was divorced for the second time. My extreme unhappiness overcame my fear of making it alone. Not only was I struggling in my marriage—my husband resented my working outside of the home—I was grinding my teeth in my sleep from the pressures of my job at the search firm. The following is a scene taken from the day that I resigned.

"Are you certain that you can't work things out?" This question came from one of the burly brothers who owned the search firm in Little Rock. I answered, "I will be 49 in two weeks. I have been married all of my adult life. Don't you think that if there was a way to stay in my marriage I would?" Too late, I heard, "Mary, you will succeed in whatever you choose to do." Now that I was leaving my husband and job, these men finally had something nice to say to me.

On my 49th birthday, with few job skills, little money, no credit or rental history, I began my life again. With the help of my college-age daughter, Marybeth, I drove my six-year-old car, pulling a trailer the 1,400 miles from Little Rock to Chicago—my hometown. That dinky trailer held all of my material possessions. However the car was in my name. I had learned something from my first marriage and divorce.

Self-Confidence

Although I did not have much in a material sense when I left Little Rock, Arkansas, I had something valuable: self-confidence. I possessed the ability to "dust myself off" after trying something and not succeeding. My heavy exposure to a brother two years older than I was, and a close relationship with my father, undoubtedly contributed to my self-confidence.

Somehow I knew that I was lucky to have had men in my life. But it wasn't until my intuition was reinforced by a research report contained in David C. McClelland's 1987 book, *Human Motivation,* that I understood why. This report dealt with the study of high achievers' lifestyles. It found that boys with a large muscular build represented a disproportionate sampling of overachievers.

The conclusion was that these boys, who were involved in competitive sports at a very early age, gained self-confidence each time they competed. Furthermore, they were encouraged to try again even if they didn't win. As a consequence, the boys grew up into confident men. Conversely, women often have not engaged in competitive sports and have seldom been encouraged to try again if they "fail." Therefore some lack the self-confidence to make even small decisions.

There is no guarantee that all boys will grow into self-confident men. Quite often society—including our parents—sabotages both sexes. We are fed a lot of no's and few do's. As adults, we play these negative tapes over and over again, often criticizing ourselves. To gain success, we must reprogram our brains—erasing these negative tapes and recording thoughts that enforce our self-worth.

Why not put a blank tape in your cassette player right now? Press "record." Say, "I like myself because _____." List all of the things that you like about yourself. Think of your appearance, personal qualities, abilities, special skills and accomplishments.

Here is what my tape sounds like:

My name is Mary F. Ivins. I like myself because I am:

• Physically very attractive, have great presence and poise, dress elegantly,

- A good person with qualities of loyalty, emotional warmth, honesty, and I am hard-working, a good listener, etc., etc., and

- I have accomplished a great deal in my life, raised six children while obtaining a BS degree, with a perfect 4.0 grade point average,

- Earned my Certified Financial Planner designation while supporting myself at a full-time job, and

- Obtained my stockbroker's license through self-study while continuing to work as a commission-only salesperson.

Listen to this tape at least once a day. Doing this will reinforce your belief in yourself. Loving ourselves—just the way we are—is very important to adopting successful behavior.

Risk-Taking

Just as we need to love ourselves unequivocally, we must understand that risk-taking is a necessary part of achieving financial success. After my second divorce and upon returning to Chicago, my bit of "tom boy" coupled with my optimistic attitude toward life allowed me to take some small risks. I use the word "small" because I still was greatly influenced by my feminine socialization, which taught that security was the ultimate good.

Each time my choice turned out well, I grew more confident. Even my so-called "failures" strengthened me as I learned that eventually everything would work out. Self-doubt was present, but for the most part I took it all in stride—accepting the consequences of my actions and not worrying about the things that I couldn't control. Again, all of this was mostly instinctive. Had I not had a trusting disposition, I would not be writing this book. Most certainly, I would not have achieved the life I now enjoy. By not taking risks, women are making a decision – one that can have distressing consequences. I learned this the hard way because I was not always a risk-taker.

At the time of my first divorce, my husband re-mortgaged our home; we each took $10,000 out of the equity. How did I invest it? I put it in the bank. Feeling ignorant of financial matters, I did not want to risk the only money I had by placing it in the mysterious stock market.

My ex-husband, however, was familiar with buying his company's stock in General Motors. At the time, it was selling at its all-time low, $29. He bought 345 shares of GM stock with his $10,000. By the end of the year, the share price had risen to almost $79. This represented a profit of over $17,000 or a return of about a 173% on his $10,000.

My money earned 8%. Taxes of 50% reduced this to 4%. Inflation of 9% reduced this further. By playing it safe, I had actually lost money. I must have had an inkling that I could do better. I began to read everything I could on investment. In addition, my second husband put me in charge of family investing. Later I will relate my negative experience with my second husband's stockbroker, which gave me impetus to strike out on my own.

After my second divorce, my ability to shoulder risk was evidenced by my decision to leave the industry that I knew, placement/recruitment, for an unknown industry, investment brokerage. Logic would have dictated that I stay with the known, however intuitively I realized that loving what you do brings success. I loved the financial world, including spending a good part of each day reading about wealth accumulation. I would combine my avocation—stock investing—with my vocation. I decided to become a stockbroker. I reasoned that if I could teach others how to make and accumulate money, I would learn too.

The timing was poor. It was May of 1982. The DOW was at a low of 740 points. (The Dow Jones average consists of 30 of the largest capitalized companies in the US. In April 1999, it reached over 10,000 points.) Back in early 1982, the large brokerage houses weren't hiring. A regional brokerage firm that did consider offering me a position ultimately refused, pointing to my low test scores on the series of technical exams given to pre-qualify prospective stockbrokers. Indoctrinated like many other women at that time, I was afraid of the complicated mathematics on the exams. I am certain that my fear defeated me. Today, of course, I am quite confident of my mathematical abilities.

So my test scores were not the highest. However, had I been a young man and not a 49-year-old woman fresh out of the kitchen, I feel I probably would have been hired. Regardless, statistics for both the brokerage and the insurance industries prove that only about one out of ten of either gender stick it out. The on-going rejection is difficult for men; it is devastating for most women.

I had been seeking a position in the brokerage business for about three months when I finally attracted a large brokerage firm. The evening of the briefing, the recruiter said, "There is nothing socially redeeming about what we do here." Since I wanted my life to count, I knew that I could not be happy in that kind of environment and refused the job offer.

Actually there was another reason that I turned down the offer. The brokerage office was located in downtown Chicago. I was fearful of the hustle, bustle and size of the city. I simply was not comfortable with so many changes in my life. I was living in Downers Grove, Illinois, at the time and accepted another "commission only" job at a nearby suburban John Hancock insurance agency. I was ignorant about insurance, but felt that I knew something about investing. I liked the fact that John Hancock was a pioneer in creating its own mutual fund system. My dream of becoming a stockbroker would have to wait, meanwhile I would have a system of stock and bond mutual funds to recommend to my clients.

My family harbored grave doubts about my succeeding. To my brother's question, "How are you going to support yourself?" I responded, "Oh, I'm going to sell insurance." He moaned. He then challenged me with "Do you know how difficult it is to sell insurance?" I again answered, "Well, I'm going to sell investments too." With that, my brother turned white.

My belief in myself was to be tested over and over again as I tried to succeed in the business world. Now loneliness was added to the fear and hard work. The insurance industry was male-dominated. I received no help from my managers. At age 49, there were no mentors for me. Not only were there no mentors—male or female—when I questioned anything, the males treated me as though I was "on the rag." I did not realize back then that a confident woman is a threat to many males.

Although I certainly struggled, I did achieve success. After the first full year in the insurance/investment industry, I had all of my insurance licenses plus my Series 6 and Series 7. The Series 6 is necessary if you are going to sell mutual funds. The Series 7 is required if you intend to sell individual stocks and bonds.

Here I must stop to chuckle a little. Even back in 1982, the Series 6 exam was on a computer. Having previously only limited exposure to computers, I was petrified. In fact, I was more fearful of goofing up on the computer than of giving the wrong answers. But I lived through the experience, and am now quite comfortable at the computer.

Not only did I gain the necessary licenses, I was the leading agent in an office of 25 men and 3 women. The Naperville paper wrote about these achievements and printed the professional photograph of myself that I had sent them. Although I could not use the self-studied-for Series 7 (General Securities) license, I had it.

I can still remember the seven-hour, written Series 7 exam taken in a stuffy classroom at a small, cramped desk at the downtown Northwestern campus. It was all that I could do to concentrate, I was so angered at the testing conditions. Added to the stuffiness (the windows could not be opened) and the small writing space (it was difficult to juggle the booklet of questions, my calculator and the computer answer sheet) was the loud chatter in the room. The monitors were holding an on-going conversation on domestic matters in loud voices all during the first part of the exam. I spoke to them about this at the lunch break. They didn't like it, but their conversation ceased during the second part of the exam. The pain endured during the test was worth it. I passed.

At this time, my normal workday lasted 18 hours. The necessary energy came from spending at least an hour each day at the local health club. In addition to aerobics, I would often swim. The pool ceiling heard me shout, "You did it! You made more money this year than either of your husbands." In 1983, I earned $50,000. I was too happy to admit to myself that I had to work the equivalent of two jobs in order to earn that much money. Success was still sweet. Now I knew that I would "make it."

My success was written about in John Hancock's in-house magazine. When the interviewer asked me how my manager had helped me, I was stuck. I thought of the time when I had asked the manager, "Why didn't you at least look at me when I was talking to you?" He had answered, "Because I didn't know if you would make it." It was obvious to me that he had not even taken the time to read my résumé. It told of the personal accomplishments I had achieved while still a homemaker. The résumé also listed the professional honors I had earned in the placement and recruiting industries. It was in that moment I realized that I had been a statistic needed to fill the minority quota for women for Affirmative Action.

To the magazine interviewer's question about what contribution my manager made to my success, I replied, "My manager allowed me to do my own thing." I added that although having control over events in our lives was good, we still prefer having the support of our superiors and loved ones. (This last statement did not appear in the article.) At times, outside support isn't there; we have to go it alone. But our belief in ourselves is all that is needed for success.

I continued taking risks. Not satisfied with my evening "kitchen table" approach to selling insurance and mutual funds that had my car slipping and sliding on ice at 11 o'clock at night, I decided to exchange my mode of operating for one geared toward the day-time business market. I joined the local Chamber of Commerce and began cold-calling on businesses. Conquering the business market was a continuous uphill battle. My John Hancock office was geared to the family market. It did not even have business forms in its supply room. Now it wasn't a case of the managers not wanting to help me; they simply weren't technically competent in the business market.

As previously stated, I was fortunate to have a healthy self-concept. I never could have chosen to take the risky route of developing a business clientele if I did not believe in myself. But even if you are somewhat unsure of your self, it is never too late to begin developing self-esteem.

The word "developing" is a great word. For we do not have to obtain our dreams in one giant leap. We can do this one small step at a time. Success is the journey and not the destination. Don't let yourself be discouraged. Look at where you came from and give yourself some acknowledgment for what you have accomplished. We do not need to be concerned with our future. We need only to be responsible for our behavior in this moment and trust our destiny to whatever you call the Force governing life.

Masculine/Feminine Energies

The self-test below is a tool given to assist you in evaluating your current behavior. The way you deal with everyday events in your life will show you how much masculine energy and feminine energy you are using. Again, masculine energy alone is not the secret; using both energies appropriately is. There are no correct answers to this "test," however your responses will show you how you think and relate to others. Keep in mind that it is a proven fact that women are often afraid of taking the risks that are necessary for successful investing. (Risk-taking is usually associated with masculine energy.) By examining the way you respond to these questions, you can begin to evaluate your tolerance for risk.

Self-Test on Masculine and Feminine Energy

1. Do you have a financial need to work?

2. Do you have an ego need to work?

3. Do you enjoy participating in sports?

4. Do you like to play games? (Cards, Scrabble, Charades, etc.)

5. How do you feel when you lose? (Be specific about your feelings and reactions.)

6. Do you prefer to watch an activity, or to engage in it? Why?

7. How would someone who's known you for a long time but does not like you characterize you?

8. Describe a social situation in which you feel very comfortable.

9. When you are faced with a frightening situation, or a situation in which you don't perform well, do you tend to back out?

10. At what point in your life were you the most popular with your peer group? What do you think was/is the reason for this popularity?

11. Do people tend to confide in you or ask you for advice?

12. If someone did not like you at first sight, what would be his or her objection?

13. If you go to the movies with friends, do you often end up seeing something you really do not want to see?

14. Do you feel that you can visit on the telephone?

15. What is your most significant accomplishment up to this point in life?

Congratulations for making it through the self-test. Again, it was designed to help you see how much you use feminine and masculine energies in your daily life. Below is some information to help you analyze your responses.

Answer Key

Your answer to Question 1 about your "financial need to work" might surprise you. In 1963, Betty Friedan's classic book, *The Feminine Mystique,* was published. In it, she exposed the issue that American housewives have various needs that are not met. Among these needs is the desire to feel that they are contributing and the wish to work outside the home. Friedan was among the first to recognize these concerns.

If you responded "yes" to Questions 2-4, it shows that you are using some masculine energy.

Question 5 asks you to describe how you feel when you lose. Do you feel that you want to try again, i.e. are you competitive? Is "angry" a word you might use to explain your feelings? Would you use the word "sad?" It does not take much imagination to realize that if you want to try it again, you are using masculine energy. A masculine reaction would be to become angry, not sad.

For Question 6, if you answered that you prefer to watch an activity, you are using feminine energy.

In Question 7, the key is the phrase "but doesn't like you." When someone doesn't like a particular woman, he or she will often describe her as having masculine qualities – such as being aggressive, self-centered, egotistical, etc. It's interesting how these same qualities in a man are often viewed by society as "good."

If you answered Question 8 by saying that you feel very comfortable in a room full of strangers, you are using your masculine energy. Or if you only feel very comfortable with those you already know, you might need to use more energy that is masculine.

For Question 9, consider that women are more likely to lack the confidence to try new things. Also, as we discussed earlier, women are less prone to trying something again if they failed the first time.

The most common answer given by women for Question 10 would be "in late adolescence." That is the time when young women exude confidence. Statistics tell us that shortly after that time many women begin to deny their own individuality and adopt a way of life that accommodates society's norms. Christopher Hayes calls this adjustment period for girls, "A Time of Clipped Wings." He further states, "When a girl stops listening to her authentic voice and vacates her inner self, the only validation left is from external sources."

If you answered "yes" to Question 11, you are likely to have leadership qualities. Others view you as a strong person.

For Question 12, if you responded that the reason someone would not like you at first sight is because you seem too self-confident, my reaction is GREAT! Self-confidence is very important to accomplishing your goals.

Regarding Question 13—A feminine characteristic is to be accommodating. Again, let me say that there is no virtue in allowing oneself to become a victim. In a subsequent chapter, I will discuss this topic further.

For Question 14, if you answered "yes," you are responding from feminine energy. Very few men like extended conversations on the telephone. Neither do I.

For Question 15, do not be afraid of "tooting your own horn." You are sure to have accomplished many things so far in your life. While you're thinking about this, why not jot down all your major accomplishments? You're likely to have many responses to choose from to select the most significant one.

Did you notice that your responses seem to indicate that you need to use more masculine energy in your life? While I was making the transition from being a full-time homemaker to a career woman, I probably used more masculine energy when making my decisions. Now I have learned to trust more and rely on my inner guidance, however I probably still analyze my decisions. Once again, a balance of energies is important. To continue to explore masculine and feminine energy, the next section will discuss left and right brain functions.

Left/Right Brain Functions

As I indicated above, the best way to make decisions is to use both masculine and feminine processes, both head and heart, or as I call it, "fact" and "feel." Our masculine energy relates to the left side of the brain, feminine energy to the right. Although each of us does make decisions based on both sides of the brain, we often use one side more than the other. Perhaps you now recognize this from doing the previous exercise.

Earlier I stated that there were no "correct" answers to the self-test. Choosing to use a certain type of energy for solving a particular problem is all right. The following story will help you to understand why.

Currently I am reading a delightful book by Eric L. Harry, *Society of the Mind*. In it, he has the computer (one of the main characters who has been programmed with feminine responses) say, "It means that I measure the world by analogy. By comparison to things I already know." The computer goes on to give an example of how the analog person (feminine) solves the problem of overfilling her cup of coffee by simply putting in less coffee the next time.

She points out that the digital person (masculine) would measure the volume of the cup, etc., to solve the problem. To her, that is using energy unwisely. No, she is not saying that solving problems through analogy, or the feminine way, is the only answer. Later she points out, "But if we're talking mechanical tolerances for your shiny new heart valve, let me suggest the model name of a very good digital computer." I think that the author gets his point across nicely, namely, using both energies is good. At times, using one of your energies is called for; at other times, using both energies, simultaneously, can be used to successfully solve problems.

On the next page is another tool to help you determine which side of your brain you favor. Examining the lists will help you obtain a truer picture of how you operate. Again, left brain functions relate to masculine traits, and right brain, to feminine characteristics.

The ability to balance your decision-making regarding financial matters with both left and right brain processes will grow as you begin to make more decisions, take small risks, and move out of your comfort zone. As Siebert says, "Through trial and error, you learn what works and what doesn't work for you. True self-improvement, self-confidence, and spiritual development come out of real life, everyday experiences, not from books or workshops."

If you are a woman learning to use more male energy, do not be afraid of appearing too masculine. Since it is still a man's world, women often need to act more like men to succeed. "For people raised to be 'good,' developing a survivor (read *successful*) style usually requires

LEFT BRAIN	RIGHT BRAIN
Dealing with one thing at a time	Integrating many inputs at once
Processing information in a linear fashion	Perceiving and thinking holistically
Operating sequentially	Having awareness without definition
Writing	Seeing whole solutions at once
Analyzing	Seeing similarities
linking	Intuiting
Abstracting	Using insight
Categorizing	Following gut feeling
Using a logical approach	Synthesizing
Reasoning	Visualizing
Making judgments	Using visual memory
Relying on mathematical axioms	Recognizing patterns
Drawing on verbal memory	Relating things to the present
Using symbols	Dreaming

learning to be more negative, selfish, angry and self-appreciating," says Siebert. Hopefully when feminine characteristics—such as gentleness, softness, and generosity of spirit—get the respect they deserve in the marketplace, women will be able to shift to more balance in their energies.

As I worked towards becoming successful, I had to stress my masculine side—competitiveness, aggressiveness, self-centeredness, etc. Earlier, being too feminine (passive), I allowed myself to become a victim. Now that I have achieved financial success, I insist that people in my life appreciate both my masculine and feminine skills. I make sure that my cooking, cleaning, decorating, companionship, social abilities, etc., be valued as well as my successes in business.

Although a primary purpose of this book is to teach women how to succeed by using more of their masculine energy, my hope is that men will read it too, including this chapter, and think about adopting some of the wonderful feminine skills—like communication. I watch in despair as my four boys struggle to relate to women. You may have heard the story of how women became such good communicators.

Since they lacked power, they had to learn how to plead their case. Men, having power, just grunted. No offense, men!

This last paragraph might make me look like a "man hater" and a "woman's libber," however even some men recognize the lack of equal power. Siebert says, "Woman . . . have managed to survive for centuries in a world where men have held official power. As a result, women have learned how to understand men much better than men have ever understood women." Al Siebert and I are "people libbers." Each of us is trying to alter tradition.

A joke might be in order here. It goes like this: A man found a bottle with a genie in it, and the man was permitted three wishes. After the genie granted the first two wishes, the man asked the genie to create a highway from the mainland to Hawaii. The genie said, "Do you know how difficult that would be?" The man thought a bit and decided to change his last request. "Well then, how about helping me understand women?" The genie responded with, "Would you like a two-lane or a four-lane highway?"

This story reinforces Al Siebert's statement. I will add my own: Women need to be patient with men. Working together, we can, as Terry Cole-Whitaker says in her great book, *Love and Power in a World Without Limits*, ". . . awaken the feminine and the masculine within all of us and return to the cosmic dance of passion and play."

Making Progress with the Right Attitude

Each of us can achieve harmony in our life by listening to our inner voice. If, as yet, you have not tapped into this inner guidance, you might try imitating the lives of successful people whom you admire. Thus you can act successful to ultimately become successful. Pick out a successful person and emulate his or her behavior. (To do this, you must first establish your own self-confidence.)

Combine this emulation with the use of the right attitude. The affirmations on the next page will reinforce your belief that all of the answers are within you.

Here's an example of how to use the affirmations. You're out skiing alone at a mountain resort. You have only skied the bunny hills before. Suddenly you find yourself on a more advanced trail. You freeze and think: *"This is impossible,"* BUT then your mind responds: *"There*

ATTITUDE ADJUSTMENT

From . . .	To . . .
This is impossible.	A Higher Power will provide all the strength I need to achieve my goal.
I am afraid.	If I do my part, life will work out.
It is not worth it.	Nothing worthwhile comes easy.
I do not know what to do.	There is a way and I will find it.
I am not smart enough.	All of the answers are within. I only need to ask for help.

---

is a Higher Power who will provide all the strength I need to get down this slope." Tapping your inner strength and the Force of the universe, you accomplish your goal.

In order to change, you must believe that all things are possible. Belief in oneself (the Higher Power within) is the secret. Stay flexible —another must for growth. When needed, change your attitude. I have given you some affirmations to use, however make up your own for only you know what the fears are that block your success.

Decisions

By listening to our inner voice, we are often guided to the right decisions. We become stronger and are able to live with more risk as we strengthen our decision-making abilities. Adding practical decision-making tools can help as discussed below.

During my second marriage, I started to learn how to invest. I began by only buying 35 shares at a time of Pizza Hut stock. This shows how afraid I was of making a mistake. I was still locked into the "security" mode. I think that the cost of the shares averaged around $25—a relatively low price. Over a period of time, I rounded up to 100 shares through two more purchases.

Because Pepsi Cola bought Pizza Hut about two or three years after I made my purchases, the price of my holding escalated. I sold the 100 shares for approximately $12,000 (I had paid about $2,500). With the proceeds from this investment, I bought "on contract" a lovely two-bedroom condominium in the same building as my rental unit. After living in this condo for four years, I was able to secure a mortgage in my own name, paying off the balloon note. Shortly thereafter, this condo became another rental property when I moved to New Jersey.

Having been strengthened by making successful small decisions, I was able to make a big decision of moving to New Jersey. I had proven to myself that I was able to survive financially. The fear of the unknown held no power. Although I felt scared—my heart said it was OK —I could survive. However, before I made the decision, I also used my analytical tool of a Benjamin T.

This was at an early stage of my growth, yet I must have known that the best decisions are based on using both the head and the heart. In case you are not familiar with the Benjamin T, I will elaborate. On a blank piece of paper, draw a huge "T." Above the left arm of the "T," put the word "For"; above the right arm, put the word "Against." Now list the reasons why the decision might be good under the word "For," and under "Against," list why it could be negative. Use a separate sheet for each decision.

If you are computer literate, use a spreadsheet for this process. Simply use the horizontal axis for each type of decision. On the vertical axis, type in the variables.

Below is an example of the spreadsheet method and it involves one of my clients. The client had recently divorced and retained the large family residence. However she was having a difficult time making the payments. She continually drew down from her savings. When I asked her how she intended to solve this problem, she responded, "Sell my house and buy something smaller, sell and rent, or take in a boarder to help with expenses." The diagram shows how I suggested she chart her problem in order to make a decision:

DIFFERENT DECISIONS				
VARIABLES	**CONTINUE AS IS**	**TAKE IN BOARDER**	**SELL HOME & BUY SMALLER HOME**	**SELL HOME & RENT**
Monthly Income				
Monthly Cost				
Effect on Savings				

Unfortunately this analytical task was too overwhelming for her. I think that she chose to do nothing, which is still a decision. In fact, she seemed upset with me for even suggesting such an exercise. Perhaps she did not want to face the reality that to "continue as is" was not a wise or long-term option. Meanwhile her savings were depleting. Although this is mostly a left-brained method, her feelings dictated her decision and lack of action. Are you allowing your feelings to dictate your behavior?

- **Are you one of the 88% allowing others to make your financial decisions?**
- **Are you one of the 75% still viewing bank-type accounts as investments?**
- **Are you keeping track of your decisions?**
- **Are you learning to tap into your inner wisdom?**
- **Is lack of self-confidence holding you back?**
- **What one action are you taking to reinforce your self-confidence?**

CHAPTER

Having an "I Can" Attitude

". . . Both poverty and riches are the offspring of thought."

NAPOLEON HILL, *Think and Grow Rich*

Our beliefs shape our actions! The way we think about ourselves is our identity. This identity is behind our behavior and creates our reality. Therefore, by controlling our thoughts, i.e., having a positive or "I Can" attitude, we can shape our reality for the good. In selecting our thoughts, we can choose self-confidence over fear, happiness over sadness, health over illness, solitude over loneliness, etc. The choice is ours. It's smart to choose wisely.

Thoughts, Energy & Form

Eventually the energy in our thought takes a form. This form is what we can see, feel and experience as our life. Therefore, through our thoughts, we create our own life. To help you understand how very important this is, here is a short jingle that we often sing during Science of the Mind services:

> *Our thoughts are prayers, and we are*
> *always praying.*
> *Our thoughts are prayers, be careful*
> *what you are saying.*
> *Seek a higher consciousness, a state*
> *of peacefulness,*
> *And know that God is always there, and*
> *every thought becomes a prayer.*

This is not a new idea. In about 180 AD, one of the pagan, humanistic Roman emperors, Marcus Aurelius, wrote in his journal, "We become the color of our thoughts." Shakespeare said the same thing: "Nothing is good or bad but what we make (think) of it." In the 1800s, the philosopher, Ralph Waldo Emerson, stated that we become what we think of all day.

Changing the way you think is not easy. It can be compared to ridding yourself of a bad habit. It takes time and effort. I call this "mental work." Unless you learn to think correctly, you will never be ready to move into your higher good. In this chapter, I will share with you several methods of changing the way you think, of getting in touch with your identity, of reinventing yourself, and obtaining the necessary attitude for success.

Desire, Determination & Discipline

You must commit to giving up the habits in your life that are preventing you from expanding and growing. To make changes in your way of thinking, you not only have to be "involved," you have to be "committed." The following analogy might help you understand this concept. The story goes that in a bacon and egg breakfast, the chicken is involved (it laid the eggs), however the pig is committed (for obvious reasons!). Commitment takes a strong desire along with determination and discipline.

The "wanting something badly enough" is the desire, or goal, which we will be addressing in Chapters 6 and 7, "Setting Realistic Goals for Self-Improvement, Parts One and Two." Now let's examine the second "d," determination. In struggling to obtain my bachelor degree, I not only had to drive on three busy expressways, I also had to use an automobile with no pickup—a very small, bright orange Vega. My first husband said that he bought the car especially for me. However, not only was the car in his name, in a color that I detested, but it was a hatch-back that was perfect for hauling the dingy he used to get to and from his moored yacht.

Fear was my constant companion as I fruitlessly floored the accelerator to get out of the way of huge trucks on the expressways. But getting out of their way was not my only bad experience. I can still remember one slushy Chicago day when the small Vega ran out of windshield washer fluid. I was on I-294—at a part where there is no shoulder. The trucks had splashed up the slush from the highway onto the windshield, blinding me. Calling on my inner Power, I made it to the next exit, my heart pounding all of the way. Now, that's determination!

At times, our determination is weakened by others' opinions. We may hear: "You're stupid to think that you can be/achieve . . ." or "You're too old to . . ." When I announced that I was going to college, my well-meaning father said to me, "You had better slow down. You are going too fast for your husband." My response: "Dad, if I am not being fulfilled and happy, everyone around me will feel it."

Don't let other people's negative comments deter you. Age, just like time, doesn't exist in the spiritual world. Too often we allow the ever-present community consciousness, i.e., the beliefs held by those around us, to convince us that we are too old to start and be enthusiastic about a new project. Let me remind you that I didn't start college until age 40 and entered the business world at age 49. If age matters, perhaps I turned it into an advantage!

A review of my subsequent accomplishments is in order. At age 50, after the first full year as a commission-only insurance/investment salesperson, I had self-studied and obtained all of my insurance licenses, the Series 6 license for selling mutual funds and the Series 7 license (stock brokerage), AND was the leading agent in our 28-person agency.

While still working every day, I next self-studied for the six-part Certified Financial Planner designation. At age 53, I became a CFP (Certified Financial Planner). At age 55, I went through the rigorous process of being accepted into the small group known as the Registry for Financial Planning Practitioners. At 60, I started my own business. Again, strong desire is the key, combined with determination and discipline. Calvin Coolidge wrote:

Press On
Nothing in the world
can take the place
of persistence.

Talent will not:
Nothing is more common than
unsuccessful men with talent.

Genius will not:
Unrewarded genius is
almost a proverb.

Education alone will not:
The world is full of
educated derelicts.

Persistence and determination
alone are omnipotent.

And an unknown author wrote:

You Mustn't Quit

When things go wrong, as they sometimes will
When the road you're trudging seems all uphill
When the funds are low, and the debts are high
And you want to smile, but you have a sigh
When care is pressing you down a bit
Rest! If you must—but never quit.

Life is queer, with its twists and turns,
As every one of us sometimes learns.
And many a failure turns about
When he might have won if he'd stuck it out;
Stick to your task, though the pace seems slow
You may succeed with one more blow.

Success is failure turned inside out
The silver tint of the clouds of doubt
And you never can tell how close you are,
It may be near when it seems afar;
So stick to the fight when you're hardest hit
It's when things seem worst that
You mustn't quit!

Others' negativism is just one example of an obstacle that can—if we let it—get in the way of our achieving our good. When obstacles appear, we would be wise to realize that they are there for a reason. I firmly believe that obstacles are placed on our path to force us to find solutions. Through this "problem-solving," we continue to grow. As we conquer lesser tasks, we are able to accomplish increasingly more difficult tasks.

These accomplishments—overcoming obstacles and challenges— contribute to our belief in self. Siebert refers to this ability to turn a

37

negative into a positive as "serendipity." He gives us a series of questions that we would be wise to ask ourselves when the going gets rough:

- Did I learn something useful?

- Did I gain new strengths? Develop more self-confidence? Become more understanding of others?

- Why can I be thankful that I had that experience? Why was it good for me?

Siebert observes: "The school of life arranges for great learning opportunities for people who react to difficulties by learning new skills."

Within each of us is the power or energy to accomplish whatever we desire. Reread the children's book, *The Little Engine That Could* by Watty Piper. Although I was first aware of it in the 1950s, the book is still in print and available. This short picture book became "dog-eared" with my constant reading and rereading to my children when I was a young mother. Even then, I had a belief in the power within—a belief in not giving up.

The story is about some toys that must be delivered to the other side of the mountain by Christmas. First a large, fancy engine was asked to take the toys over the mountain. It refused the job as it did not want to get dirty. Then a plainer but equally strong engine was asked. This engine refused because it claimed that the job was unworthy; its dignity would be insulted. Finally the littlest engine in the yard was approached. He said, "I think I can." It was his belief in Self that allowed him to go over the mountain with the heavy load of Christmas toys for the boys and girls. Yes, he was puffing, but he kept saying, "I think I can, I think I can, I think I can . . ."

This is just one of many examples of how thinking or believing can change your life. In fact, it is belief that replaces fear. Faith (also known as belief or trust) and fear are really just opposite ends of the same spectrum. Here's an exercise to illustrate this point. Picture a line. Fear is far to the left, faith is far to the right. It is the absence of fear that allows us to have faith (belief); conversely, it is the absence of faith that causes us to fear.

No, this is not my original idea. This is one example of polarity or oneness first stated by a very wise man, Hermes, who lived in ancient Egypt. Under Hermetic principles, everything exists in relationship to something else. Good and evil, black and white, light and dark, the South Pole and North Pole, faith and fear. Thus the concept of polarity or oneness. Hermetic principles teach that there is no such thing as duality.

A little background on Hermes. In Egypt, individuals who seemed to possess special powers were made into gods. Thus, Hermes became one of Egypt's heavenly gods (Mercury with the winged hat), son of Jupiter (Zeus) and the goddess Maia. According to conjecture, Hermes was the forerunner of mathematicians and astronomers.

Those who espoused what later became known as the Hermetic principals—such as polarity—formed the Hermetic Society. As our western society developed, and along with it Christianity, the ancient mysteries contained in the Hermetic principles became very unpopular. So in the Middle Ages, the Hermetic Society became a secret society. Today those people interested in learning about the meaning of life are once again studying these ancient mysteries including polarity.

I stated earlier that commitment to self-growth involves desire, determination and discipline. I have been discussing determination. Let us now look at the third "d"—discipline. The old adage that says, "No gain without pain" is close to the truth. In order to regenerate yourself, i.e., to "reinvent" yourself and to develop your true identity, it is necessary to throw out all the old assumptions. This can be a painful process, requiring tremendous discipline. Reinventing "you" will also involve questioning, rethinking, reexamining, reevaluating and creating, on a conscious and a subconscious level, a new belief system.

Who Are You?

On a consciousness level, you can start the process of reinventing yourself by using the following self-discovery exercise. Take out 10 index cards, and write this incomplete statement on each one:

"My name is_____

and I am a/an_____.

Now, without thinking, quickly write down your answer to the question "Who am I?" on each one of the cards. An example might be:

"I am a fat person." Here, again, there are no "right" answers. Just be spontaneous because then you will have the best representations of what you "feel" about yourself. Don't intellectualize!

Arrange these cards in order of priority, i.e., which one best describes how you feel about yourself, and then number them. If you need more than the 10 cards, that's OK. Use as many as you need. Now, turn the cards over. On the back of card #1 write:

"This 'I am' is first because _____."

Do the same process with each of the cards. After you have completed the cards and thought about them for a short time, pretend that someone else wrote these cards. On a pad of paper or in your computer, write down the answers to these questions:

1. What do these cards tell me about this other person?

2. What things are most important to her/him?

3. What things would this person enjoy doing with her/his life that she/he is not doing now?

4. How would I recommend that this person spend her/his life if she/he were told that she/he only had six months to live?

Have these cards and the above exercise sent a message to you? Do you feel that you may need to rethink how you feel about yourself and how you are living your life? Quite often we block our higher good because we hold onto erroneous beliefs about who we are.

This exercise was adapted from the book *Working Smart* by Michael Le Boeuf, Ph.D. I highly recommend Le Boeuf's book. It was attracted into my life many years ago. The main message is getting what you want out of life by being focused. Absorbing Professor Le Boeuf's ideas from *Working Smart* helped me to become more organized. A subsequent book of his, *Imagineering*, assisted me in further developing my creative side.

Getting back to our beliefs about ourselves, it's unfortunate that our early religious indoctrination often fosters erroneous thinking in this regard. If you were raised Catholic, as I was, you might need to replace the false belief that you are born in original sin. My Baltimore catechism classes taught this dogma yet also stated that we were "made in the image and likeness of God." However this additional teaching didn't go far enough. What was left out was that in the beginning there was only God, therefore he made you and me out of Himself.

We all share God's divinity, no matter how you perceive Him. My personal belief is that since God is on the invisible plane, He works through us to showcase His qualities. Of course, man has been given a special gift, which is choice, and he has often chosen a less than perfect life. God is impartial, therefore we must always be aware of what we are asking for (read *choosing*). Furthermore, it is my belief that the "I" in the expression "I am" is God or the Higher Self within. Therefore the "I" can only represent perfection. As a possessor of God's qualities, such as beauty, joy, goodness, happiness, etc., anything that is evil, including sin, cannot be part of us. Is it possible that you are giving God/your Higher Self a false identity?

Replacing Negative Character Traits with Positive Ones

On the next page is a list of negative and positive character traits that I'd like you to review. This list was first developed by spiritual leader, Jack Boland and is reprinted from the book *Master Mind Goal Achiever's Journal 1999*, © 1999, used with permission from the publisher, Master Mind Publishing, Inc. Start by finding a negative emotion that you are experiencing on the chart, then disclaim it with: "This is not my truth." Next, find the offsetting positive characteristic and claim it with: "My truth is _____ . (Work the positive character trait into your statement.) Doing this process will reinforce the positive aspects of your belief system. Note that some of the positive traits, such as acceptance, honesty and the ability to laugh at one's mistakes, are further discussed in the next chapter on adopting winning personality traits.

Unlike various other authors, I do not think it is necessary to go back into the past to find out why we hold certain beliefs. Today is a new beginning. We can start changing our attitude right now. Concentrate on your emotions. The present moment is all that we have to work with.

Actually, time is an earthly concept. There really is no such thing as time or space. We are points in the Universal Mind. As such, we

MAKE YOUR CHOICE POSITIVE	
Negative Character Defect	**Positive Character Trait**
Fear	Faith/trust
Procrastination	Action now
Rationalization	Reality
Rejection: self and others	Acceptance
Guilt	Self-acceptance/forgiveness
Dependence	Self-reliance
Self-pity	Dramatize (Laugh at self)
Resentment	Forgiveness and love
Intolerance	Tolerance
Impatience	Patience
Envy	Praise (Rejoice in another's good)
Egotism	Open to others/considerate
Jealousy	Live and let live
Manipulation	Total honesty
Alibis	Truth
Impulsiveness	Control
Egocentrism	Awareness of others' needs
Selfishness	Generosity/being loving
False pride	Humility

embody the past, present and the future. Our past, i.e., our memories, create an idea. This idea strongly held, truly believed in, becomes our reality (future). Remember, whatever you focus on—with emotion—will show up in your life! It is said that the thought is the engine and the emotion the fuel.

While you are eradicating negative emotions, don't stay rigid—accept opposite traits in your personality. When studying survivors, Siebert often noticed that they contained paradoxical character traits. At first, he was certain that possessing conflicting character traits—being sad and happy, stingy and giving, etc.—would cause confusion. He found, however, that some kind of hidden radar guided these individuals. They trusted in this guidance, and as a result, they were calm and peaceful at all times.

In fact, different situations often call for some "negative" behavior. Flexibility in our behavior in every situation is paramount. This flexibility was called for one day when my oldest son, then five, arrived home from school 15 minutes late. When I questioned him, he responded that the bus was just late.

However, Michael—like his mother—is honest to a fault. I pursued the questioning. He finally admitted that he and his friend, Billy, had stopped off at Dunkin' Donuts for a treat. Because I strictly followed our pediatrician's advice and most sweets were forbidden in our household, Michael felt that he had to lie. Inwardly I was laughing, however I had to make myself get angry. I scolded him by sternly saying, "Lying is not acceptable behavior, Michael." This is just an example of how we can choose our emotions to fit the situation.

Subliminal Tapes

Although it is easier to work on the emotions that we realize we have and are at the conscious level, at times, our feelings about something are in our subconscious mind. Our parents, grandparents, neighbors, siblings, classmates, etc., could have placed these negative thoughts or feelings there. I had a wonderful Irish grandmother who was very religious but superstitious at the same time. "Sing before breakfast, cry before night" was one of her favorite sayings. Not meaning to, I'm sure, she was squelching some of my childhood enthusiasm with that sentiment as well as planting a negative subconscious thought in my mind.

Dealing with eradicating negative thought patterns on the subconscious level might require the use of subliminal tapes. These tapes contain positive messages meant to replace/negate destructive beliefs. They work because they are recorded at a frequency lower than what we can hear at our conscious level. This is necessary because our conscious minds often deny the truths contained in these tapes. Usually the subliminal messages are recorded beneath a louder natural sound such as ocean waves breaking on the shore.

You might question the effectiveness of these tapes. Like the "old" me, you may intellectualize everything. It took me a while to accept the idea that subliminal tapes work, but then I started seeing results in my own life. Here again, trust comes into play. Along with resisting the idea that subliminal tapes work, it can be difficult to believe that our subconscious plays a part in our behavior. Many times we are not even conscious of faulty thinking.

I once heard a presenter discussing subliminal tapes at a group meeting. He told a story of such tapes being tested on three groups. The first group used tapes featuring the sound of the ocean and positive messages had been recorded at a low decibel level. The second group had tapes of the ocean sounds, without the subliminal messages included. The third group had tapes with the messages and the ocean sounds plus a script of the subliminal missives. Can you guess which group benefited the least? It was the group with the script! This was because their conscious minds could not accept or believe the positive messages.

Since my first exposure to subliminal tapes, I have grown in my understanding of why they work. Now I realize that our power comes from our belief in something – even subliminal tapes. How else can we explain verifiable research that shows that in certain studies individuals given placebos (sugar pills) got well just as quickly as those given medicine. Use whatever tools feel right for you in order to deny any negative thoughts—conscious or subconscious. Just get started!

Do you allow negative thoughts to stay in your conscious/subconscious mind?

- **What did you learn from doing the self-discovery exercise, "Who Am I?"**
- **Did you recognize in yourself any of the negative or positive character traits listed?**
- **Do you believe that making attitudinal changes is like changing habits, i.e., that it takes time and effort?**
- **Have you committed to the three "d's?" Have you memorized them? (Desire, determination and discipline)**
- **How much time are you devoting to changing/altering your belief system?**
- **What is the most important thing you are trying to change?**

CHAPTER

Adopting Winning Personality Traits

"Life is not fair—and that can be very good for you."

AL SIEBERT, PH. D., *The Survivor Personality*

The game of life is like a poker game. It is not the hand that we are dealt, rather it is the way we play the hand that counts. Often we view adversity as a negative. But we learn more from the things that the world views as mistakes than we do from our successes. Along with believing strongly in ourselves and having an "I Can Do" attitude—characteristics that were discussed in the last two chapters—there are certain other personality traits that constantly show up in the lives of successful people.

I have been a prolific reader all of my adult life. My reading has always included biographies, autobiographies and fictional biographies. We can learn much about winning personality traits by reading about the lives of successful individuals, those who have left their mark on society. Unfortunately I was initially influenced in my choice of books by what the media had to say. However guidance is always present. Somehow I was eventually led to books that presented a different view of famous people. Currently I am reading Ronald Reagan's autobiography. In it, Reagan is revealed as a much different person than what I had become to believe was his persona. Another person's life that had been hidden from me was that of Harry S. Truman.

Over time I discovered that it is unwise to allow the media to bias my opinion about famous people. In fact, the first winning personality trait that I present is that of being non-judgmental. In addition, I list nine other qualities of being honest/fair, accepting, non-victims, self-rewarding, fun-loving, playful, resourceful, creative and thankful. Do you have these winning personality traits? If not, get to work.

Being Non-Judgmental

Leaders allow people to be who and what they are, never judging another's behavior. And if you do not judge, then you do not gossip. It wasn't until I was 27 that I learned these lessons.

Here is the story of how I learned this. As a young mother with small children, I delighted in visits from a friend named Agnes. She was so colorful and witty in her conversation. However one day I suddenly realized that her talk consisted mainly of speaking negatively about her other "friends." Not only was I allowing myself to become a part of all of this backbiting, I knew instinctively that my family most certainly was a topic of her barbs too. I severed that relationship.

At the same time, I took a good look at my own belief system. Things seemed to come easy for me at that time in my life. I often thought or said out loud, "Why can't they do things like I do?" I realized that I was no better than Agnes; I was being equally judgmental. From that moment on, I decided to only worry about my own behavior. I recognized that I did not have the answers for everyone in my world—only for me.

Being non-judgmental includes not demanding perfection of ourselves. We are so busy doing things right that we fail to do the right things. I call this "analysis paralysis." Often women are guilty of this. They research something to death but never act. Leaders are quick to make decisions and have learned to live with those choices that don't turn out. Again, women, in general, have not been socialized to dust themselves off and go out and compete again when something does not work. They are afraid of making mistakes. This is another reason why it is necessary to include more masculine energy in our lives.

Women are prone not only to expect perfection in themselves, but in others as well. Then, when the other person's behavior does not measure up to their expectations, they allow themselves (read *choose)* to be distraught. The truth is that no one—our children, husband,

46

lover, boss, fellow worker, etc.—causes our unhappiness. We do it to ourselves.

This point became very clear to me when I read the book, *Your Erroneous Zones,* by Wayne Dyer, Ph.D. While this book, Dyer's first, was very meaningful for me, his subsequent published writings have been even more influential on my growth. In fact, the gift of his wisdom at a recent lecture that I attended remains in my thoughts. One of the important things he said was: "If you have a choice between being right or being kind, choose kind." By being non-judgmental, we are choosing kindness.

Being Honest & Fair

Choosing to be kind is an example of being fair in our dealings with others. If we follow the Golden Rule that is a part of every religion, we will always treat others kindly. The Christians express it this way: "Inasmuch as you have done it to one of the least of these my brethren, you did it to me." (Matthew 25:40) Earlier I stated that there is no such thing as duality; each of us is a part of a whole. These Golden Rules support this belief by stressing that what we do to others, we are doing to ourselves. When in doubt regarding how to behave, ask yourself, "Would I like to be treated that way?"

Along with not being judgmental, we need to practice honesty and integrity in all that we do. According to the great spiritual leader Ernest Holmes in his wonderful book, *The Science of the Mind,* "Every man knows right from wrong, in its broadest sense." It is my belief that dishonesty of any kind stops the flow of our good.

Recently I was talking to someone about manifesting her good. I knew that she reads positive-thinking material and has a fair grasp of the metaphysical principles. However what I learned during this conversation was that she allowed her accountant to falsify her tax reports. Since there is a natural law of reciprocity, i.e. "we reap what we sow," sooner or later this cheating will come back to her. For now, she is in a state of confusion; the good that she desires is eluding her.

My integrity was tested while working in the insurance industry. Like most women, I asked a lot of questions. I was told, "You don't have to know that, just sell some insurance." I probably gave my prospective clients more information than they wanted or needed, however it was the only way that I could act. I felt that I would rather give them too much information than leave something out that they might need before committing to the sale.

Think about integrating the principles of honesty, fairness and integrity into your mission statement (main goal statement) for your life, your professional efforts or business. When starting up my own financial planning firm, I composed a mission statement that read: "To assist Individuals and Business Owners to obtain their financial goals in a fun and elegant manner—always putting our clients' needs first."

The following is the corporate statement of Beyond Words Publishing, Inc., of Hillsboro, Oregon.

Inspire to Integrity
Our Declared Values
We give to all of life as life has given us.
We honor all relationships.
Trust and stewardship are integral
to fulfilling dreams.
Collaboration is essential to create miracles.
Creativity and aesthetics nourish the soul.
Unlimited thinking is fundamental.
Living your passion is vital.
Joy and humor open our hearts to growth.
It is important to remind ourselves of love.

This mission statement speaks volumes. It is well-written as well as inspiring. Cynthia Black and Richard Cohn founded Beyond Words Publishing, Inc. in 1984. Today, it is a flourishing publishing company with 12 full-time employees. Some of the titles that Beyond Words has published: *Money and Beyond, Winning with Love* and *You Can Have It All.* Its Internet address is www.beyondword.com.

One of the important contributing authors to Beyond Words Publishing, Inc. is Arnold M. Patent, who lives in California with his wife and three children. He has spent the last 15 years writing books and conducting seminars on the basic principles of the Universe. Recently the beautician at my mother's nursing home shared with me how greatly Arnold M. Patent had influenced her life. She sent me one of Beyond Words Publishing, Inc.'s flyers which featured Mr. Patent.

I am not certain why Arnold Patent and his work have been attracted into my life; only time will tell. However, I do know why Beyond Words Publishing, Inc. was attracted. I had written for permission to use its corporate statement in an earlier book. I was not only given permission, I was also given encouragement. The success story of Beyond Words Publishing, Inc. is proof that by giving we receive, which is discussed in the following chapter, "Developing a Money Consciousness."

Being Accepting

Besides being honest, we would be wise to be accepting. The manner in which we accept/reject and learn from the things and people attracted into our lives determines our growth and maturity. In *You'll See It When You Believe It,* Wayne Dyer, Ph.D., talks about qualities that contribute to spiritual growth. He says that acceptance of what shows up in our lives and a belief that we are a part of a larger plan are traits of self-actualizing, successful people. Although he experienced extreme poverty during his childhood—actually he was shunted among at least five foster homes before the age of ten—he never felt deprived. He accepted without question whatever showed up for him.

I can identify with what he says about acceptance. As a child of the Great Depression, I went around with the toes cut out of my shoes. I only had "hand-me-down" clothes. When my aunt Gladys took me to buy my eighth-grade graduation dress, she was aghast when she saw that my slip was made out of a flour sack and that I was not wearing a brassiere. I was 5'7" and weighed 137 pounds. She was definitely being kind when she uttered: "Doesn't your mother realize that you are growing up?" As Dyer says, "Kids don't give much thought to being unhappy or feeling deprived."

Again, examine what shows up in your life. Is it something that you can change? Is it something that you cannot change and must accept? However, being accepting, as we shall see below, does not mean that we allow ourselves to be victimized. There is a BIG difference.

Refusing to Be a Victim

When I divorced my first husband, I received none of our "retirement nest egg." This retirement fund had been built up by my husband's contribution of 10% of his gross salary, matched by his company with 50 cents for each dollar up to 6%. The fund contained General Motors stock and US Savings bonds. I also did not receive any of my husband's pension. However I was used to doing without, therefore I was not disturbed.

When I divorced my second husband, I was treated very unfairly once again. As stated earlier I received nothing from the sale of our homes. Although I had spent countless hours in "sweat equity" on improving both homes, which increased their values, the lawyer for my second divorce said that I was not entitled to any of the proceeds. He stated that my second husband had made the original down payment on the first home and its built-up equity was used for the down payment on the second home. As a woman of the '50s I expected the man to handle all of the financial dealings—like making the down payment on a home. Besides, at the time, I had very little money, $10,000. Again, being financially ignorant and wanting out of the relationship, I accepted this unfair distribution. Perhaps some of you can identify with this?

Not loving myself enough, I allowed myself to be victimized. I accepted the unjust divorce settlements. Lucky for me that I believed then—and still do—that there is a good reason for everything that shows up in our lives. Instinctively I harbored no resentment. Now I realize that had I carried resentment, I would have stopped the flow of my good. And as my son, Bill, said, "Mom, if you had been dealt with fairly, you wouldn't be writing this book." Is there any resentment in your life that you need to clear out? Do it now.

However not being resentful does not mean that we continue to allow ourselves to be victimized. In fact, whatever we choose our behavior to be will cause the other person to act in a certain manner. There is no virtue in being a victim; without a victim, there cannot be a tyrant. Knowing this, I no longer accept ill treatment or "put-downs" from anyone.

During the 1950s, it was easy for women to allow themselves to become victims. Earlier I cited an article on a 1950s Home Economics textbook. Recently I received a humorous e-mail message containing similar information. Someone had added a postscript: "You call this humor?" This book supported the belief that a woman's sole purpose in life was to be a good wife and mother. My life showcased exactly what this book advocated. Not only did I exemplify the perfect wife and mother—treating my husband as though he was a king—I also contributed countless hours to volunteer work. Yet I was not entitled to my own Social Security.

This imbalance of power still exists. Back then it fostered the women's movement and later caused many divorces in the US in the 1970s—including my own. Today it continues to influence the shockingly high divorce rate in the US. Not only did the marriages of the 1950s suffer because of this power imbalance; it is my belief that the boys, who are now men, raised in these male-dominated homes continue having difficulty treating women as equals.

Although women today are better at expressing their needs, society's expectations haven't changed that much. Currently a woman is expected to be a wage earner while still performing all of the traditional woman's duties. Not only are women not treated equally with regard to home responsibilities, Hayes says that women are still not treated as equals when it comes to household financial decisions. He says, "Paradoxically, women are now expected to be wage earners, but gender roles within the household still often leave men with the power and control. Women need to realize that a by-product of earning one's own money is the right to do more than supervise the checkbook and pay the bills; they need to have a say in how that money is spent and invested."

Being Self-Rewarding

Part of the reason why more women do not share in financial decisions is that often women do not want to "rock the boat." They do not want to appear too aggressive. They are nurturers to everyone but themselves. They usually put their needs/desires last. Women need to reward themselves—to put themselves first.

Usually it is necessary to remind ourselves to do this, since we can feel guilty about spending any money on things we want just for us. But rewarding ourselves need not cost a lot. While raising my six children and working with a budget of $80 a week, I rarely bought anything for myself but I still rewarded myself.

During the day, I would wave at a book that I had placed on the coffee table in the living room. I'd say, "See you tonight!" I looked forward to spending an hour or so before bedtime with the book. At times the book was one of the shortened classics that came with the *Books of Knowledge* purchased for—but seldom read by—the children. Sometimes it was a book borrowed from the library.

Even if what we want does cost some money, so what? The "nudge" to do or have something is right. It is termed "divine dissatisfaction." All action is good. We would be wise to identify with Frank Lloyd Wright. He said, "Take care of the luxuries and the necessities will take care of themselves." He also said, "I have no remorse, guilt or regrets about the way I've lived my life." How do you reward yourself?

Being Fun-Loving

We not only feel guilty if we reward ourselves, we also feel guilty if we're having fun. Let your heart lead. If I had allowed my practical side to rule, reading for pleasure would not have been allowed. I had six children! However, choosing to take time out of my busy life for some relaxation (reading) was intuitive. I was acting on a need. Contrary to some people's belief, being needs driven is a positive—not a negative. If we listen to our hearts, our intuition will point out our needs.

In our Western civilization, we are often too busy to listen to our biological needs; being non-productive is seen as bad. Many of us were indoctrinated with this Protestant/Judeo work ethic. Erasing the work-ethic tape was difficult for me. At age 43, I enrolled in a group beginning-piano class at Eastern Illinois University. I remember sharing with my good friend, Hermy, who is from Austria where music is so important, that I felt guilty doing "nothing" while practicing the piano. She replied, "You are not doing nothing; you are feeding your Spirit." Thank you, God, for putting Hermy on my path!

Today, at age 66, I no longer feel guilty when I am having fun. I am once again learning to play the piano. I budget at least an hour each day for practice. I am pleasured from hearing the simple classical pieces improve. One of my goals is to be able to accompany the family as they sing Christmas carols when we gather at the end of the year. Currently I am working on "owning" every Christmas carol in a beautifully arranged piano book by Eric Steiner.

Yes, my neighbors might wonder at hearing Christmas carols in the middle of summer, but nothing stands in the way of achieving my goals. Another goal is to someday play the deluxe edition of "Over the Rainbow," which was recently attracted into my life. You will understand why after listening to one of its refrains:

Somewhere over the rainbow, skies are blue,
And the dreams that you dare to dream really do come true.

Being Playful

Learning to be playful is different from being fun-loving. Playfulness is an attitude that we have toward life, and it's particularly important in regard to how we react to upsets and our own mistakes. It also involves our approach toward our daily life, and avoiding taking things too seriously.

Learning to laugh at our circumstances is a must. A really good "belly" laugh is the best kind. Recent scientific studies have proven that it is both psychologically and physically healthful to laugh. When we laugh heartily, we take in oxygen, which releases healing chemicals. My ability to laugh was assisted by the 12-year experiencing of Rich, my ex-significant other. When I first met Rich, I took everything very seriously. I had been living on my own for about four years when Rich came into my life. Subsequently I followed him to New Jersey where he had transferred. We lived together for 10 years.

Rich has a whimsical nature and gives playful names to everything. His blue Volkswagen was "Rufus," my brown Audi was "Junior." My new Audi was named "Cream Puff" since I was always anxious that nothing happened to it. My bike was "Jezebel" or "Jezzy" for short; his bike is "Mephistopheles." I'm not certain why Rich gave this name to his bike, however the name is from Johann Wolfgang Von Goethe's poem, "Faust." While doing the research, I came upon these words of advice by Mephistopheles to Faust:

Do thou the like, and follow me,
All unembarrassed thus and free,
To mingle in the busy scenes
Of life, and knowing what living means.

Interesting! Being unembarrassed and living life to the fullest would describe Richard. Again, thank you, God, for enriching my life through experiencing Rich.

Now not only am I able to laugh at things in general, I also am able to laugh at myself. Some of the things that I do really seem stupid, but

I accept them as a part of who I am. In fact I can now even laugh at myself in frightening situations. Shortly after moving back to Chicago, I volunteered to pick up my mother at the busy O'Hare International Airport. I kept circling the airport, trying to find a sign that read "Parking Garage." I learned later that no such sign exists; the authority uses the term "Main Airport" to indicate the public parking garage. At any rate, on one of my circles, I turned too soon and wound up on the wrong side of a six-lane highway, driving against traffic.

As I listened to a cacophony of horns and saw the flashing headlights, I asked myself, "How could you be so stupid!" but then I suddenly found myself laughing. Instead of getting flustered, I was able to think calmly. I made a U-turn and that was that. This story illustrates the idea that being childlike and playful does not mean being childish. In order to become self-realized, we must be spontaneous and learn to live in the present moment just as children do.

Besides laughing at myself, I have also introduced whimsical items around my home. A while back, I purchased an elf cookie jar. The face has two huge dimples, and you can't help but laugh when you look at it. I have named the elf "Danny Dimples." I greet him each morning, and we both laugh! More recently, while visiting Oberammergau, Germany, I bought a cuckoo clock with a whimsical appearance. I not only enjoy seeing the clock in my home, it also gave me a reason for a big belly laugh when I first used it. I wondered why the cuckoo was not appearing, but then discovered that I had forgotten to unlock the cuckoo's door!

Hopefully you already do laugh and do not struggle as much as I did. I have spent most of my life believing that I had to overcome all obstacles by myself. During the time I was striving to build up my business, I was very stressed and tense. You can imagine how difficult it was to become successful in a male-dominated industry, entered into at almost 50 years of age. Now I realize that by struggling, I prevented my good from showing up sooner.

Today I am much less serious and know how to relax. Living in this splendid environment in Chicago with a calming view of the lake from every window of my luxury condo has helped tremendously. In fact I have experienced a shift in my belief system. I no longer fight for what I want. I listen to my intuition, take action when needed, and wait patiently for the results to show up in my life. I have adopted the universal law, called by various names—the law of least effort, an economy of effort, etc., etc.—that states that by doing less, we accomplish more.

Don't be discouraged if your belief system doesn't buy into this axiom immediately. However you might learn from Nature. It does not struggle. The tree does not try to become a tree; it just is. The sun does not try to shine; it just does. The stars do not try to twinkle; they just do. And babies don't try to be blissful; they just are. Giving up the struggle will free you to enjoy each moment and allow you to just "be."

Being Resourceful

The subject of being resourceful is repeated often throughout this book. Often it is life's obstacles that cause us to be resourceful. Fortunately challenges have always inspired me to work harder. However it wasn't until recently that I recognized that having something to push against is beneficial to our growth.

In fact, while attempting to get this book published, I constantly ran into people telling me that it couldn't be done. My first such experience bears retelling because it illustrates my point of resourcefulness being a stepping stone to success.

Included in the first steps of launching a book is writing a "query" letter to see if an agent is favorable to your concept and would take on the promotion of your book to a publisher. I sent out about 15 of these letters to literary agents. From a local college, I received an invitation from a part-time literary agent to come in for 30 minutes. At our meeting, she did everything possible to discourage me. At the end of our talk, she said, "If your book is published, let me know," and I responded, "Not 'if,' you mean 'when.'"

Upon relating this story to my neighbor Vicky Hill, she broke up laughing. She asked, "I wonder what she thought you were on?" But it was my turn to laugh when I woke up in the middle of the night with a response to one of the literary agent's statements. At our meeting she had said, "It is not what you know, it is who you know that counts." I wished I had thought to respond, "Well, I know 'God' and who could be more important?" Unknowingly, I'm certain, this literary agent demanded that I become resourceful. This book is the result.

Being Creative

Being resourceful and being creative are closely related. The ability to be creative or "make do" was forced upon me at an early age.

My father believed that as soon as his children became teenagers, his financial responsibility ceased. I held numerous jobs during my teen years, lying about my age before I was 16. These various jobs contributed to my ability to manage time and money while allowing me to continue living a full life. I not only worked at least 30 hours a week; I made most of my own clothes. I also bowled in two bowling leagues, roller-skated twice a week (I had my own precision skates and knew how to do all of the dances), dated frequently and was on the Honor Roll at my high school.

It is said that "necessity is the Mother of invention." Perhaps this is true. I do know that when we create something beautiful out of something that at first seems of little value, we feel good inside. Again, intuitively, I knew this. I was always challenged but never discouraged about my need to create nice things for myself. When I was a teenager, linen flats were a very popular shoe style. I would have the natural-colored ones dyed to different colors—red, aqua, yellow, etc. Then I would buy yarn to match that color. Using half of a large oatmeal box, I would crochet a cover for it, ending with about three additional inches. In the additional part, I would place holes in the crochet for the drawstring. This drawstring was made by doubling the yarn and crocheting with a single-crochet stitch. Then I lined the inside of the box with a matching colored material. I always felt dressed up when I wore my dyed linen flats with the matching colored purse.

The ability to make do and create continued into my married life. My "new" clothes consisted of altered discards given to my mother-in-law by her wealthy employer. I would take these expensive clothes completely apart and redesign them to fit my figure. This exposure to elegant clothing contributed to my "money consciousness." This is an example of turning a negative into a positive.

Not only did I not have any brand new clothes during my first marriage, my home was completely furnished with good used furniture. With creativity, Murphy soap, Old English, and Guardsman furniture polish, I turned these discards into lovely furniture. By being resourceful and creative, I managed to create harmony and elegance in spite of seeming lacks.

Later I was able to purchase a few new things with the money I earned by doing AMVET calling from my home. AMVET stands for American Veterans and is or was a service organization that had resale shops located throughout the nation. Each week, it took me approximately six to eight hours to make the usual 300 calls needed to get 60 women (my quota) to say that they would put out a box of discards. My husband scoffed at the $30 a week that I received. However it was the start of my independence. I saved up my weekly paychecks until I had enough to buy some of the things I wanted for my home. One of these new things was quite elegant—a crystal chandelier from Austria. How I loved cleaning it!

Being Thankful

It would be great if we remembered to be non-judgmental, always honest and fair, accepting of life as it comes, non-victims, free of hatred or resentment, conscious of our need to reward ourselves, open to becoming playful and having fun, as well as being resourceful and creative. All of these character traits are good, however the most important one is thankfulness.

Adopting a regular routine of listing all of our many blessings—in a litany or sonnet of thanksgiving—causes us to become even more thankful. The act of doing this releases tension and feelings of discouragement and disappointment. We stop feeling sorry for ourselves. I suggest you do this once a day, upon rising in the morning or before you go to bed. You can either mentally note what you are thankful for, or write the items down in a special journal.

Too often we are caught up in the mundane everyday world and forget to be grateful. Recently the hymn, "Amazing Grace," has been attracted into my world. I am told that this was composed by a man who had been a slave trader most of his life. During that time, he probably shut out God and the natural, positive Force of life from his awareness. I too was blind to the natural positive flow of life when I was so engrossed in becoming a financial success. I forgot that everything I needed would be provided and that I did not have to struggle. I failed to see how my life was naturally graced with blessings every day.

I love playing a simplified version of "Amazing Grace" on the piano. Its lyrics are very inspiring:

> *Amazing grace! How sweet the sound*
> *That saved a wretch like me!*
> *I once was lost, but now am found,*
> *Was blind but now I see.*

Being as happy and joyous as I am, it is only natural for me to greet each new day saying, "Thank you, thank you, thank you." Before I go to sleep, I give thanks for all of the blessings of that day and for all of my life's blessings. Take the time to examine your life. Do you recognize where Grace has touched your world? Here is where thankfulness is called for.

- **Do you judge others?**
- **Are you too hard on yourself?**
- **Do you still use the "s" words, "should" and "shouldn't?"**
- **Are you honest in all matters?**
- **Are you accepting of the things that you cannot change?**
- **Are you allowing yourself to be victimized?**
- **What type of rewards do you give yourself?**
- **Can you "play" without feeling guilty?**
- **When did you last have a good "belly" laugh?**
- **Do you welcome the challenge of being resourceful and creative?**
- **Do you daily recite a litany of thanksgiving for your many blessings?**

CHAPTER

Developing a
Money Consciousness

*"It (money) is Intelligence forever finding new outlets
for its own creative action."*

RAYMOND CHARLES BARKER, metaphysical speaker and writer

The attitude that we hold towards money is so important that I
have devoted an entire chapter to it. We must develop a "money
consciousness." By this I mean that we need to realize that money is
not a commodity to own, rather it is a "good" that we can use to live
more fully. We must view money as fluid, as part of this great pulsat-
ing Universe—not as something static—an amount of money in the
bank, an investment, etc.

As we learn to trust completely in the bountiful Universe, we act
differently. "See and feel money in your hands," says Napoleon Hill in
his book, *Think and Grow Rich*. He is reminding us to act the part of
already being rich and prosperous. Rehearsal—i.e., becoming the person whose role we are enacting—is the key to success.

The renowned prosperity teacher, Catherine Ponder, says that
everything is attracted into our lives, either consciously or subconsciously. She suggests that we affirm that we already have money. "I
have all of the money that I need right now" is a good affirmation.
However, for the magic to work, you must truly believe that the
Universe will provide all that you need, and if you are experiencing
lack of any kind, it is only an appearance—not real.

Also, Ponder points out that we need not feel guilty about having
more than others. Just as there is abundance in all of Nature, we have

59

a right to be prosperous, accepting nothing less. This thought is repeated over and over again by writers and speakers of prosperity subjects. They also give additional advice:

- Give of your energy—including talents and money—to receive,

- Open your mind to receive,

- Develop and maintain a positive attitude about money,

- Congratulate and give compliments to others,

- Take responsibility for your own financial life, including making certain that you have credit in your own name even if you are married.

Giving—Money, Energy & Talents

In every encounter, ask yourself, "What can I give to this person?" At times, it is money; at other times, it is your energy or your talent. Probably the most difficult lesson for each of us to learn is that to give is to receive. Instead of worrying about giving too much, worry about giving too little. Deepak Chopra, a well-known spiritual teacher, says that we should never go anywhere without a gift. He further states that this gift can be quite simple—a flower or a comment praising the host/hostess, etc. It is giving something of ourselves that is important.

The North American Indians understood the meaning of giving/receiving. I once read a book, *Hanta Yo* by Ruth Beebe Hill, which is based on writings recorded on buffalo robes. It described one of the ways these Indians showed their deep trust in the bountiful Universe. They would empty their teepee of everything they owned, setting the items out for their neighbors to take. Because their fellow tribesmen knew that receiving and giving are the same thing, they gave back. In fact, these same Indians believed that a worthy gift had to be one that was difficult to give. By the following day, the family that had emptied its teepee of all material possessions had more and better of what they had previously. Wouldn't it be great if we could develop this kind of trust!

Opening Your Mind to Receive

We often hear that "It is better to give than to receive." However it is my belief that the receiver is more important. Here, in the US, individuality and independence are indoctrinated into each of us. Too often we give an immediate "no thank you" to any offer of assistance. Just remember that without a receiver, there can be no giver. Again, it is good to give, however we also need to learn how to receive.

At times we do not feel worthy of the good that we receive. The belief in self-denial with a hope of a reward in the hereafter is a part of many religious teachings. If some good comes our way, we doubt that it can continue. This "waiting for the other shoe to drop" attitude keeps our good at bay. Have you ever heard yourself say, "This can't last"? This indicates that your mind is not truly open to receive, i.e., you don't feel worthy.

Along with allowing ourselves to give others the opportunity to give by becoming receivers and not feeling guilty, we must be consistent in our thinking about money. Picture the Universe as a giant computer. In the morning, you affirm, "I now have the beautiful automobile that I have been envisioning." In the afternoon, you say to your coworker, "You know, I really can't afford a new car." Like a reprogrammed computer, the Universe becomes confused. Don't do this! Claim your new car by saying that you already have it. Thank your Higher Power. End this affirmation of your prosperity by saying, "This is for the greater good for all concerned."

Developing & Maintaining a Positive Attitude about Money

Part of being open to receive our good is developing and maintaining a positive attitude towards money. This means always—not sometimes —speaking positively about it. Raised in a frugal family, I often heard money spoken about in a negative way. Even today, it is difficult for my mother to be non-critical about the way I spend my money. She always introduces me as "The daughter who acts like she has money."

Recently when I gave her a present of expensive pajamas, she remarked, "Nothing but the best, hmm?" Of course, she does not know that she is telling me that I have developed a positive attitude about money—a great money consciousness! In metaphysical jargon, we say, "Fake it until you make it." Yes, we must always see ourselves as having all that we need and want.

Learning this was not easy for me, but I eventually did and so can you. I spent much of my childhood counting pennies. I probably even felt poor. However my attitude toward money began changing during my Oak Park teen years. At Oak Park/River Forest High School, I was exposed to wealthy children from River Forest, Illinois. They wore cashmere sweaters, pleated wool skirts and leather penny loafers. In an effort to dress like them, I started shopping in the better stores. Perceiving that I could not afford full price, I shopped the sales at the high-class, expensive retail shops. The discounts were substantial, often a 50% reduction. I was able to buy fabulous outfits at a fraction of their retail price.

Note the word "perceiving." The reality is that we always have enough money; it is our belief in lack that brings it into our lives. I am certain that learning to shop for value contributed to the "somewhat correct" attitude I held toward money most of my life. Today I feel that I have developed the "correct" attitude toward money. This includes never thinking or talking about "lack" of any kind and trusting in the Universe to supply all of my needs—including my monetary ones. On every check, I write "GIMOS" (God Is My Only Source). I believe the positive Force of life is always with me.

Congratulating and Giving Compliments to Others

Not speaking of lack includes congratulating others on their good fortune. We must be genuinely happy for another person's success. Stop and think of all of the incidents that would call for congratulations. The obvious ones are birthdays, weddings, births, etc. However, there are many more, including academic achievement, job promotion, new apartment or home, better or new furniture, better or new clothes, etc., etc. The list really is endless when we start to think expansively. And, best of all, a compliment doesn't cost anything.

Before I understood fully how important it was to my growth, I probably hesitated before giving a compliment. Now as soon as I think of something nice to say, I share it. In my building lives a woman whose name I don't even know. Often I would see her on the bus, in the lobby getting her mail, or somewhere else in the building. She always wore a sour face. One day we were on the elevator and she forgot to punch her floor. I laughed and said, "Guess that you thought that the elevator could read your mind." She laughed too. Immediately I spoke my thought, "You are so pretty when you smile." She continued to smile and does so each time we meet.

Taking Personal Responsibility for Our Financial Lives

Along with adopting the belief system that holds that all good—money included—is our right, we need to take personal responsibility for our own financial life. Often women are guilty of "stinkin' thinkin'." We suffer from a Cinderella Complex, believing that someone else will take care of us. I believed my first marriage would last forever—it didn't. Furthermore I believed my second husband would always take care of me—he didn't.

One doesn't have to be married to suffer from a Cinderella Complex. Often single women believe that a Prince Charming is just waiting in the wings and will sweep them off their feet, taking care of them for the rest of their lives. Perhaps they aren't aware of the statistics:

- One out of two marriages ends in divorce.

- The average age of widowhood is 56.

- Women outlive their mates by an average of seven years.

- More women who can't find the right man are refusing to get married.

While women continue to improve their economic situation—especially in the US—you can see that statistics show we still have a long way to go in our thinking. We need to be realistic about financial matters, including insisting on having our own credit when we are married.

In 1979, more than four years after my first divorce and while still in the second marriage, I purchased a real estate investment using my $10,000 initial divorce settlement as a down payment. Although I had received my total divorce settlement by then—approximately $30,000—I did not want to use all of it for this investment. I decided to apply for a mortgage. Since I was still a full-time homemaker without my own credit history, I could not get a mortgage in my name. My second husband had to co-sign for the mortgage. However, despite the fact that the mortgage had both our names on it, I insisted that the deed be in my name alone.

My second husband was not happy about my decision, but I held out. I could still remember how helpless I had felt at the time of my first divorce. After 23 years of marriage, I had absolutely nothing in my name but the marital home. In fact, the only divorce settlement that I received came from my part ownership in the family home.

At the time I bought my investment condo, I was satisfied with my second marriage. But I think that subconsciously I must have felt that I could always live in the condo if my marriage ever went sour. Three years later, I was divorced. However I did not move into my condo, as it was rented and the lease was not up.

I called the condo association and was given the name of a woman who managed 12 investment condos in the same Downers Grove complex in suburban Chicago. After my second divorce, I had no job, rent history, or credit (I learned this later), however this unknown woman rented me a one-bedroom condo based on a phone conversation. Providence was shining on me. Thank you, God, for putting this trusting woman, Kay Cahan, on my path.

I was not aware of how helpless I was. After I moved to Downers Grove, Illinois, I tried using "my" credit card. I was told, "You have no credit of your own. Your husband's name is on the account." While working at the search firm, I had purposefully applied for credit in my name alone. I can only assume that the credit-card company did not consider my commission-only employment worthy of credit, and without my knowledge, it had added my second husband's name to the new account. Are you certain that you have credit in your own name?

Not possessing credit in my own name or a job for over three months made the adjustment to living as a single, self-supporting woman more difficult. But I was fortunate to have some of the second divorce settlement put aside for emergencies. I was not only supporting myself but my college-age daughter and a 28-year-old unwed-mom daughter as well. Beds were everywhere—including the kitchen. When the lease was up on the one-bedroom condo I had rented from Kay's employers, I decided to purchase a two-bed-room condo. It was in the same building and Kay was again the manager.

I still marvel at my optimism. I had just started working for John Hancock and reasoned that I needed a second bedroom to use as a home office. Conventional financing was not open to me. However, because of Kay's trust—and I suppose because I had shown that I was a responsible renter—I was able to buy on contract. The mortgage stayed in Kay's employers' names, but I assumed the payments of $850 a month. I also committed to paying them back the entire price—minus my down payment—in five years.

My friend, Hermy, was horrified at the risk that I was assuming. "Put more money down and reduce your payments" was her advice. From some hidden wisdom, I replied, "Well, I have some money in the bank. I would rather put less down and have a better tax advantage. Besides, if I'm short a few hundred dollars, I can always go to the bank." Of course, by taking on a debt that I had to pay back in a systematic manner, I established credit. After four years, I qualified for my own mortgage and bought out my contract. I had come a long way financially. Not only was I successful in my career as an insurance/investment salesperson, my investments were appreciating too.

Although it may seem that I was irresponsible to take on so much debt, it was a sign that I had expanded my consciousness. I was no longer afraid to take calculated risks. Even if you are in a "safe" (does one exist?) marriage/relationship, you would be wise to experience risk-taking. Establish your own credit by taking out a loan in your own name and successfully pay it back. Isn't it ridiculous that wives are often not given any money of their own to use as they please? I feel strongly that a working married woman would be wise to deduct a portion of her check before contributing to the family pot. And it would be smart for a "stay-at-home Mom" to receive an allowance that is hers alone, one that she is never asked to account for. Also, single women need to establish a solid credit history, and to use credit with creativity as well as prudence.

- Do you feel that you have a "money consciousness?"
- Do you give gifts that are difficult to give?
- Do you experience guilty feelings when good shows up in your life?
- When was the last time that you volunteered?
- Do you monitor your thoughts and words – especially about money?
- Do you ever hear yourself say, "I can't afford that?"
- When someone you know has good show up for them, are you genuinely happy for them?
- Have you accepted responsibility for your own financial welfare or are you guilty of "stinkin thinkin"?
- Do you have credit in your own name? Do you use it wisely?

Setting Realistic Goals for Self-Improvement Part One: Life Goals

"The people who get on in the world are the people who get up and look for the circumstances they want."

GEORGE BERNARD SHAW, Irish-born author

Looking for the circumstances that we want involves setting goals and doing whatever is necessary to achieve them. In *Simple Abundance,* Sarah Ban Breathnach says, "The world needs dreamers and the world needs doers. But above all, the world needs dreamers that do." She is reminding us to follow our dreams, but at the same time to have an action plan. The Bible puts it this way: "Faith without good works is dead."

Global Goals

One of the characteristics that Siebert found in people who consistently appear to be living successfully was that they wanted everything to run smoothly. They wanted peace for themselves, their loved ones, strangers and, most of all, for the world. In other words, they not only have personal goals, but global goals as well. Global goals are those that benefit the world. To be successful, one would be wise to establish global goals as well as personal goals. In fact, if your goals include a selfless idea—like contributing to world peace—you have a better chance of succeeding.

I am reminded of a story about a mother who after a long day at work was trying in vain to read the paper. Her little boy kept interrupting her. In desperation, she tore out a page of the paper that had a picture of the world on it. She then ripped the page into 12 pieces. "Here," she said, "put this puzzle together." In no time at all, the boy was back with the completed picture. The mother was amazed. "How did you do that?" she asked. "Simple," he replied. "One side had a picture of a woman on it. The other side had a picture of the world. I knew that if I could put the woman together, the world picture would come together too."

Personal Goals

This story illustrates that when we achieve a peaceful state for ourselves, automatically our state of mind has a powerful influence on the whole world. We can develop this peaceful state by achieving some important personal goals. These include:

- Improving our appearance,
- Developing a social support network,
- Integrating spirituality into our life, and
- Creating an environment that feeds our spirit.

All the above goals will be discussed in this chapter. In particular, in a latter section of the chapter, I will provide some powerful tools to help you work spirituality into your daily life.

These personal goals must be combined with monetary goals, which is the topic of the next chapter. Another important personal goal, education, will also be discussed in the upcoming Chapter 7 in terms of learning about financial issues.

Another way to look at the personal goals we need to set is to address the body, soul and mind. The scientific world is finally discovering that our psyche is interrelated with our body. Becoming "whole" or "one" is the answer to success in all areas of our lives.

A simple tool that I always carry in my wallet will help you establish goals in all areas. Pictured on one side of the card is a small can with red lettering saying: "Success Comes in Cans—Not in Cannots."*

---

* The message on the can is the registered trademark of Joel H. Weldon & Associates, Inc., P. O. Box 6226, Scottsdale, Arizona, 85261. Phone: (480) 948-5633. Fax: (480) 443-0425. This company specializes in corporate seminars. The cards are available.

Printed alongside the picture of the can is:

Build a Better You
"Your task: to build a better world," God said.
I answered, "How?
The World is such a large place,
so complicated now;
And I so small and useless am,
there's nothing I can do."
But God in all His wisdom said,
"Just build a better You."

(The other side reads:)

My 30-Day Goals

By_____19___, I Will

1)_____

_____
PERSONAL GOAL (JUST FOR ME)

2)_____

_____
FAMILY GOAL (WITH THOSE I LOVE)

3)_____

_____
MONETARY OR BUSINESS GOAL (IN THE WORK I DO)

Appearance

Oftentimes we have to improve in other areas of our lives before achieving financial success. Our personal goals might include projecting success with a great appearance. Whether it is losing those extra ten pounds or seeking advice in how to dress, do it NOW! You owe it to yourself to look your very best. Statistics have proven that leaders are quite often attractive people. They project energy and are viewed as winners. Improving our appearance can help give us the confidence to improve in other areas of our lives.

Aspects of appearance to be addressed include weight, dress, poise, features and voice.

Weight

If you have ever lost weight, you know the feeling of rediscovering your youthful energy. I am a lifetime member of Weight Watchers. I feel that this organization teaches us how to eat properly. It forces us to change our eating habits, giving us more energy. My adult weight has always been in the area of 138-158 pounds. Although at times I have worn a size 10 comfortably, a size 12 seems to be more me. Not only do I look and feel better at my normal weight, I also can wear the lovely wardrobe put together by a wonderful image consultant that I attracted into my life. I believe it is important to set a realistic weight goal that is not extreme.

Dress

When I started my career at age 49, having been in the home all the previous years, I had no professional wardrobe. Perceiving that I had little money, I purchased my professional wardrobe at a resale shop. Later I bought new clothes in brown or beige, thinking these colors gave me a professional image. Although I thought that I was fairly good at choosing the correct clothes, I still had a goal of learning how to dress stylishly and elegantly.

Learning to dress with style and elegance came as an offshoot of a bad experience. After working for the Naperville insurance agency owned by John Hancock for four years, I moved at age 53 to the East Coast. Looking back, this had to take courage, however having courage in the face of change and challenge is a part of who I am. I decided to take a chance, as I wanted to experience living on the East Coast, had no family responsibilities at that time, wanted to learn the sophisticated side of the insurance business, and was romantically involved with a man named Rich who had recently relocated to New Jersey.

I did everything I could think of to establish a New Jersey client base. One thing I tried was joining a professional networking group. Only one professional in each category was allowed to join the group. I was rejected because the stockbroker felt that my work overlapped into his business. I considered myself a financial planner, but his wishes prevailed and my membership was rejected.

It happened that the leader of the networking group dressed beautifully. I complimented her and mentioned that I had always wanted to find someone who would teach me to dress properly and stylishly for business. She said, "I have just the woman. Her name is Irene Tanner. She is an image consultant and lives on the Upper East Side of Manhattan."

Over a 10-year period, Irene taught me how to dress well and built an exceptional wardrobe for me. She started out by doing my colors. The color groups she used were named after the seasons of the year. I was a true winter—my color group included reds, bright pinks, vivid blues and purple. Yet the entire wardrobe that I already owned was beige or brown. Not only was beige not my color, the styles I had chosen—like button-down collars and dirndl dresses—were wrong for me too.

Irene traveled by train from Manhattan to our western New Jersey suburb. She did what she termed a "closet review." She made three piles: "Keep," "Think about," and "Get rid of!" The pile labeled "Keep" had only three items! This closet review was followed by the development of a shopping plan. The main purpose of this plan was to locate a store that had a sufficient quantity of the type of clothing that Irene thought suitable for me.

Irene went with me on shopping day. Guessing that my wardrobe did not project the "Goddess within" (one of Irene's favorite phrases) but also realizing that I might have to transition slowly, Irene had selected a rather conservative suit and two non-conservative ones. When I put on the conservative suit, I was not excited. But my continence glowed when I put on the less conservative suits—here was the "Goddess within" that Irene was looking for!

With Irene as my wardrobe consultant, I had to do more than adjust to different types of clothing. I had to adjust to buying very expensive (for me) clothes. Before we bought the two suits, our very first purchase was a silk scarf for $55. I was shocked at the price. I had been used to spending that amount on a blouse or even a dress. When Irene suggested that I buy Bruno Magli or Ferragamo pumps, I replied, "I'm not spending $250 on a pair of shoes." But eventually I learned that the more expensive clothing gave me added self-confidence.

Irene and I normally bought groupings at the beginning of the season in order to be able to purchase the pieces that we wanted. That meant that I paid full price for the clothes. However from Irene I learned to look for value, to buy clothing that would stay in my wardrobe for years. In addition, I learned what colors and styles best suited my personality. Now I have a great wardrobe.

Irene is no longer an image consultant; currently she is founder and president of Suited for Success, a non-profit organization that works with economically disadvantaged women to teach them how to dress and act during the job interviewing process. Thank you, Universe, for placing Irene Tanner, Manhattan, New York, on my path.

Poise

Along with dressing well, one needs to be poised. As we become more calm and peaceful, we become more poised. This is another aspect of self-realization. We need to recognize and believe that within ourselves we will find the Power to accomplish whatever we want. We also need to realize that we don't have to have perfect looks. We must learn to love ourselves—accepting who we are. Depending on others to determine our self-worth is unwise. A little ditty that I learned while attending the Science of the Mind church helps me to keep this in mind.

I love myself the way I am,
There's nothing I want to change,
I love myself the way I am,
There's nothing I want to rearrange.

Repeat out loud as often as possible: *"Peace and Poise Produce Power and Prosperity."*

While you are working on consistently projecting poise, constantly remind yourself to relax. Take a few deep breaths when you feel agitated. Repeat, as I do, "Divine Right Action Is Taking Place Right Now." As mentioned earlier, it is usually by appearance that we judge others and are judged. However there is a Divine plan in all of this. If we are wise, we will stay calm and listen for cues as to what we should be doing. Doing this will create peace in our environment. Again, I am convinced that if we would just learn to "be" and stop all of the action and chatter in our lives, we would project harmony. Not only would we project harmony, good of every kind imaginable would flow in and around us.

In addition to the spiritual aspect of poise, there are some other practical things that I learned to do. For instance, my eighth-grade teacher, a nun, was very critical of my posture. I was at my adult height —5'7"—and most of the boys came up to my armpits. In an effort to appear shorter, I slouched. The nun used to hit me in the back and say, "Stand up straight." She also suggested that I check my posture in the plate-glass windows as I walked by. Although I did not appreciate Sister Mary Clarence, BVM or "Clarabell" (our nickname for her) at the time, I do now.

The other thing that I think contributes to poise is knowing that you always look your best. I make certain that everything in my closet is mended and clean—ready to wear, using shoetrees for my shoes and boots. I also demand that I keep orderliness in my surroundings. Yes, at times, my environment gets cluttered— especially when I'm focused on finishing a project. However my spirit can only stand a small amount of this. We both feel better when things are picked up.

Features

Loving ourselves the way we are doesn't mean that we can't choose to help Nature along. We can improve on our features. Having uneven coloring in my front teeth, I had them bonded, which evened out the tones. I started wearing contacts at age 62. Much earlier, I had tried unsuccessfully to wear contacts. My severe astigmatism had always prevented me from succeeding. But the Universe attracted an ophthalmologist into my life who said that I would see better if I wore contacts. Furthermore he said that all that was required was that I had to have a strong desire to wear the lenses and go through the necessary uncomfortable adjustment period. You guessed it; I really wanted to get rid of those glasses. Now I delight in not having my glasses slipping down my nose when I play tennis and in not dealing with my ski goggles clouding over.

Since returning to Chicago, I have continued improving my appearance. I had laser treatments around my mouth and chin to remove some of the hereditary and ex-smoker lines. In addition, my "old" eyes were changed into "young" eyes when the plastic surgeon removed some of the excess skin in my eyelids. Thanks to a personal body trainer, I no longer have sloping shoulders. Thank you, Universe, for Ezra Kazam, M.D. (ophthalmologist), Jerome Garden, M.D. (dermatologist), Neil Fine, M.D. (plastic surgeon) and Mike Wozniak (personal trainer).

Voice

Since the majority of people pay more attention to how we sound rather than what we say, it would be wise to develop a pleasant speaking voice. If you are not fortunate to have a nice voice, consider taking some elocution lessons. Talk into a tape recorder. Read aloud.

I once knew a man who was raised in Bronx, New York. Knowing that society does not consider a Bronx accent cultured and that he would never make it to the top in the advertising industry with this accent, he worked tirelessly to develop a neutral sounding voice. When I knew him, he had earlier risen to the top in a New York ad agency, and had then become the successful owner of his own advertising agency in New Jersey.

A fun way to learn how to speak properly and in front of people is by joining a Toastmaster group. There are currently more than 8,500 Toastmaster clubs worldwide, representing more than 60 countries. Toastmaster members are individuals from all walks of life—plumbers, carpenters, teachers, salespeople, psychologists, accountants, etc., etc. Each club member is given a certain type of speech to prepare to present in front of his or her group. The group then critiques the speech based on a written form. Since the individuals in the group possess different levels of speaking skills, there will always be someone in your club that you can learn from AND your ability will teach others at the same time. To find a club near you, call 1-800-993-7732 or visit the Toastmasters International Website at www.toastmasters.org.

Social Support

The Toastmasters clubs are just one example of a way to develop social support for obtaining your goals. When I was in sales, I learned of a method to obtain sales leads that I would like to share. Form or join a group of individuals from different professions. This is the type of group that I mentioned I had tried to join in New Jersey. Each group member is responsible to furnish leads that the other professionals might use. I had this in mind when I later formed a professional network that was registered under the name of The Business Network of New Jersey. The idea was to create a Master Mind group, described by Napoleon Hill as the "Coordination of knowledge and effort, in a spirit of harmony, between two or more people, for the attainment of a definite purpose." The primary purpose of the group was for lead generation, however at the same time my goal was to create a positive support group.

The professional networking group that forced me to start my own organization did me a favor. I am certain that this organizing experience had a huge impact on my growth. For the twice-monthly meetings, I chose an elegant hotel in nearby, prestigious Summit, New Jersey where a gorgeous breakfast buffet was served daily. We ate in a side room off of the main dining area. What fun it was to get dressed up every other Tuesday. How enjoyable it was to share the companionship and support of the group.

It was within this group that I obtained many of my business leads. Also, I used the services of several of the members, including the skills of a very talented, giving human being and graphic designer, Mikel Cirkus, who created my business brochure as well as my business cards and stationery. Each professional represented a single industry. There was an attorney, an accountant, a banker, a travel agent, an actuary (one who designs pension plans), etc. I served as the President for two of the four years that I was a member. I remained with the group, finally leaving when a new element of individuals took control. Our philosophies were different as was exhibited in their choice of a meeting place—a diner.

The reader might take the last statement as negative. It is not. I have found that when I stay in a group whose philosophy is continuously at odds with mine, no growth occurs. This is not a "put-down." Each of us is on a path to perfection. It is unrealistic to believe that everyone is on the same rung of the ladder. Before I leave a group, I do some mental work and go within for the direction. I have found that if we go against our "feel" (read *heart)*, we suffer.

Spirituality

To maintain perspective on your life and handle challenging times, it's important to develop a way to integrate spirituality into your life. Another benefit that came out of my rejection from the networking group in New Jersey was my introduction to a great spiritual leader, Reverend Gwen Gillespie. She was to play an important role in my becoming. Here's how it happened.

As mentioned earlier, when I moved to the Garden State, I was desperate to find prospects to turn into clients. My wardrobe consultant, Irene, allowed me to send invitations for one of my financial seminars to her friends and clients. My presentation was held at the fashionable Doral Tuscany Hotel in mid-Manhattan. I reasoned that Irene's clients had money since they, like I, were paying $100 an hour for her expertise. At the time, I was not aware of the other side of Irene. She was heavily into metaphysics and had many friends—not clients—who had not as yet realized their prosperity dreams.

These were the ones that attended my first seminar. I had spent approximately $2,000 on setting up and promoting the seminar and ended up losing money. But I certainly enjoyed the experience and learned quite a bit. Knowing that it is necessary to repeat an action in order to be successful, I decided to give another seminar to the same group. It was while preparing for this one that I became so discouraged. Sitting alone in my office, on the verge of crying, I called Gwen, whose name and number had been given to me by one of the metaphysical attendees of my prior seminar.

I literally bawled into the phone, "I am so alone." Gwen's response was firm. "You are not alone. God is with you." I was ready. From that moment on, I have never been alone. God (the Universe's Divine Intelligence, my Higher Power) is included in everything that I do. It is my constant companion. Over the next 10 years, I continued to grow spiritually. I am so thankful that Gwen was placed on my path. This is yet another example of how what at first seems like adversity really is not.

For a time I attended the Science of the Mind services conducted by Gwen in Princeton, New Jersey. From my home, I would drive approximately 25 minutes on Sunday mornings to the services. Much of my philosophy was developed during that period. In addition to attending the Science of the Mind services once a week, during my 20-minute drive to and from my office in Morristown, New Jersey, each day, I did mental work. I would start by affirming: "There is one life, and that life is God, and that life is my life right now. There is a Power in the universe that I can use for good. All that would cause doubt, confusion, fear, anxiety, worry, unhappiness, anger, resentment, jealousy, competition and envy (here, I name the negative traits that I feel cause me the most trouble) is uprooted from my consciousness. My consciousness is God's consciousness and as such is filled with love, beauty, peace, contentment, joy, happiness, laughter, harmony, orderliness and perfection."

I then added, "Therefore I claim and affirm perfect health, prosperity and abundance, loving and fulfilling relationships, and creative energy."

I went on to elaborate how each of these things would manifest in my life. I added all of the details so that there would be no misunderstanding as to what my needs and wants were. However I left some room for the Universe to do the creating by adding that I would accept "the equivalent or better."

Then I thanked the Universe for already giving me what I had requested. I added that all of this is "for the greater good of all concerned." I would then say, "I claim this good and state that since I have placed it in the Divine Mind, it is already mine. All that I need to do is wait for it to show up." I followed this with what I call my "litany of thanksgiving." This is a listing of all of the wonderful gifts that I have already received from the Universe.

Put simply, our affirmations should contain approximately five steps.

1. Join with and identify with the Oneness of the Universe - the God Power. This includes claiming the God Consciousness as your own.

2. Speak into that Power. Be exact on what you desire to show up in your life. This can be the thing that is a top priority in your life right now. In other words, it can be in just one area. For instance, you might want a new home. You can then describe exactly what you would like to find in that home. Remember, the more you can envision and the more you can feel this thing in your life the better.

   Later, as you become more sophisticated with this method of manifesting things in your life, you can address all of the areas of your life as I do.

3. Accept—i.e. know—that you deserve what you have asked for. Know that you would not have the desire unless it was also God's desire. Since you are One with this God Head, it cannot be any other way. The desires of your heart are God's desires.

4. Expect your good and believe wholeheartedly that it is already yours.

5. Give thanksgiving for the good that you have asked for and release it into Mind. When you are saying "thank you," you can add "for this good or the equivalent or better." What you have in mind sometimes differs from what the Universe desires for you, however what you will receive is never less than what you asked for.

In order to manifest your good sooner, write each of your desires down in a notebook. Carry this notebook with you at all times. Refer to it at least three times a day and particularly right before you go to sleep. Again, don't be concerned. Release and trust the Cosmic Force to answer your needs. Remember, after planting the seed, it is counterproductive to be pulling it up all of the time to see if it has developed into what you put into Mind.

It should also be noted that prior to speaking my affirmation, I endeavor to raise my consciousness through breathing exercises as well as chanting. As each of us must find our own way with this, I refer you to the Bibliography where you will find books with additional information on these tools as well as others.

Environment

Along with learning to look and sound our best, surrounding ourselves with positive people, and practicing spiritual principles, it is important to create an immediate environment that feeds our Spirit and allows us to grow emotionally. Yes, our personal surroundings do play a big part in our ability to expand and grow. Although, as stated earlier, money was often scarce, all of my homes have been lovely, warm and inviting.

Along with having a lovely home, intuitively I knew that I must have a great view of Nature wherever I found myself. When I lived in New Jersey, I hired a contractor to replace the very small dining room windows with an eight-foot sliding door that opened out to an acre of forest in the back. When I started my own business, I did not hesitate to pay top dollar for a lovely office with a gorgeous view on the 14th floor of the tallest building in Morristown, New Jersey. Today the views from every window in my two-bedroom corner condo are breathtaking. I have an east and south view of Lake Michigan and great views of the Chicago skyline and Grant Park.

Choosing views to Nature was in answer to an intuitive need. Later, after reading *Love, Medicine & Miracles* by Bernie Siegel, M.D., I came to realize that answering my needs has kept me extremely healthy. Siegel points out that his patients who had windows in their hospital rooms improved much more rapidly than those who were without windows. Nature feeds our Spirit.

Take a look at your home and office. Do they reflect your Spirit? Have you added personal touches—things of beauty and elegance that make you feel good? You do not necessarily have to spend a lot of money, but don't buy anything that makes you feel like you don't deserve the best things in life.

Thoughts & Goal Achievement

After I was divorced for the second time and forced to survive alone, I became so caught up in the material world that I neglected my spiritual/intuitive side completely. My actions mirrored society's belief that we need to focus on striving hard to achieve success. Later I learned to balance the technical and spiritual aspects of life.

It took me most of my life to learn how to do this. Although for approximately 10 years I had been trying to use the metaphysical principals, doing a spiritual treatment each day, my faith was not fully developed. Faith did not come to me until about three years ago. At that time, Reverend Michael C. Rann, one of my spiritual teachers, remarked: "We should focus on what we wish to receive from the Universe, *knowing* (trusting) that we will eventually receive that which we give our attention to." I was ready to listen.

He used the metaphor of a torpedo. He said, "A torpedo moves from side to side as it is honing in on its target. However, once it fixes on its target, no matter what the target does, the torpedo will reach it." I now realize that my life process has been like this torpedo and continues to be so. For something to materialize, we must believe that it will. We must be able to grasp the things that are always present but that we are not ready to see.

Now I have become more aware of the way things show up in my life. For example, 15 years ago, I had pasted a picture of a lakefront condo on my office workstation. In the intervening years, I probably didn't give this much thought. However, when I moved back to Chicago, my dream was to live on the lakefront. A day after moving into my "dream" condo, in one of those flashes of revelation, I realized I had rented the very unit pictured in the real estate ad that I had pasted up so long ago.

Emerson said that everything and every person that ever existed still exists. However we are not able to realize them until we have a need. I had to move to New Jersey, to start my own business, and to be able to pay over $1,500 a month in office rent before I could move into my good. Earlier than that, my mindset told me that I could not afford to live my dream. It had taken me 15 years to be ready to accept/see this reality.

Just as it took 15 years for my dream condo to materialize, it has taken an equal amount of time for this book, which I have come to believe is also a part of my life script, to be born. Fifteen years ago, I was offered the opportunity, but I wasn't ready. I recently came upon a part of a sentence that I had underlined at that time while researching this book. It is a quote by Spinoza: ". . . in the gathering, I am happy, and pass my days not in sighing and sorrow, but in peace, serenity and joy." His words, "peace, serenity and joy," aptly describe my current state of being. I now understand that nothing—people, events, writings, etc.—show up in our lives haphazardly. I believe, like many others, that there is a Divine plan.

After stating our goals and picturing what we want to show up in our lives, all we need do is listen and wait. Our inner guidance will let us know our part—what action to take. We only have to do our part—not the Force's part. When we learn to trust completely, we begin acting on automatic pilot. We become Unconsciously Competent and are headed for the life that we want!

To help you understand and adopt this state, I offer this analogy. When learning to drive a shift-automobile, there are four phases we go through:

- Unconsciously incompetent
- Consciously incompetent
- Consciously competent
- Unconsciously competent

Before we start learning to drive a shift automobile, we are *unconsciously incompetent*. Once we start to learn, we become *consciously incompetent*, constantly grinding the gears. Painfully we learn to put our foot on the clutch and shift at the same time; the result is less gear grinding. Constantly keeping our mind on what we are doing, we become *consciously competent*. After we have driven for a while, suddenly we don't have to think about what we are doing; we simply do it. We have reached the stage of being *unconsciously competent*. This fourth stage could be stated another way; we are now in "sync" or "going with the flow."

In the next chapter, Part Two of "Setting Realistic Goals for Self-Improvement," we will look at determining your *financial* goals.

- **What are your life goals?**
- **Do you hold a vision of your good?**
- **What makes you get up each morning?**
- **Do you remind yourself at all times to stay determined and disciplined?**
- **Are you balancing or integrating both of your energies: masculine and feminine?**
- **Do you take/make the time to stop the chatter in your mind in order to listen for direction?**
- **Are you able to completely trust in your Higher Power?**

Setting Realistic Goals for Self-Improvement Part Two: Financial Goals

"Back of all of this demand for new and better things, there is one quality which one must possess to win, and that is definiteness of purpose, the knowledge of what one wants and a burning desire to possess it."

NAPOLEON HILL, *Think and Grow Rich*

Now that you have learned about setting and achieving goals in other areas, it is time to establish some of your financial goals. This chapter will discuss becoming educated about financial matters, dealing with technical information, hiring experts to support your efforts, and looking at your long-term money goals. A chart and a worksheet at the end of the chapter will help you start thinking about what it will really take to secure your future financially.

Officially we do not address the Success Formula for Financial Independence until the following chapter, but this is really where you start to incorporate it into your financial success strategy. You must commit to setting aside a certain portion of your income each month in order to accumulate the wealth needed.

Becoming Educated about Finances

After the financially disastrous ending of my first marriage, I was determined to obtain knowledge of financial things. I sought out books, magazines, newspapers, financial reports, etc., to raise my understanding of financial issues. As with everything I do, I worked hard at learning how to invest. If I was interested in a certain company, I sent for its 10-K. This report must be filed each year with the SEC (Securities and Exchange Commission). It contains information about the company including its mission statement and business practices.

I also enrolled in the pre-requisite courses I needed to qualify for acceptance into the MBA program at Eastern Illinois University, a college 37 miles from where I lived with my second husband. The year before, at age 42, I had received my bachelor degree in Secondary Education, with a major in Spanish, from Northeastern Illinois University. My double major had prevented me from choosing any business courses.

Before becoming eligible for the MBA program, I first had to earn 24 business credits. Eventually I did earn 21 business credits, however I dropped out before taking the requisite calculus course. That September, my husband decided that we would vacation in Spain for two weeks. Realizing that I could not make up the work in the difficult calculus course, I gave up on the idea of taking the class. But the business courses that I did finish contributed hugely to my ability to self-study and pass both the Series 7—General Securities—exam and the six tests for the Certified Financial Planner designation. My MBA goal is yet to be realized.

During the time that I was taking the pre-requisite courses, I kept house for my second husband and my two youngest children. Just as in my first marriage, I continuously sewed draperies, roman shades, valances and curtains, painted the walls inside and outside the house and wallpapered—using chintz for the bathroom walls. I even made time to sew some lovely tennis clothes, which I still have. My high energy and persistence allowed me to accomplish a great deal. I created a lovely home while pursuing an MBA, driving approximately 80 miles a day to take the classes.

The point of this story is that having a busy life does not prevent us from getting what we want. What stops us is not wanting something badly enough. A common complaint of today's busy woman is: "I don't have time for all of this learning." My answer is that we can find or make time for anything we really want. You too can learn whatever is necessary for your success with your financial goals. Combine your desire to succeed financially with some or all of the practical tools below:

- Financial magazines

- Business section of newspapers

- Books

- Seminars

- Course work

- Investment clubs

- The Internet

I am aware that you may have little interest in these tools. However you are reading this book for a reason. It would seem that one of your dreams is to take charge of your financial life. To make my dreams come true, I had to learn how to invest. I had to use my masculine energy to assimilate this technical financial knowledge and act on it. As stated throughout this book, each of us has two types of energy— male and female. For success with our finances, we need to use both.

Dealing with Technical Matters

It often helps to remember that each person who comes into our life is there to teach us something. I certainly must have had a lot to learn from engineers as many of the men in my life have had a background in that area. The list of engineer-type thinkers and those with degrees in engineering is lengthy: My father (inventor), brother (electronics engineer), first husband (mechanical draftsman), second husband (civil engineer) and Rich, my "posselq" (people of the opposite sex sharing living quarters) for 10 years (computer engineer).

I am certain that my exposure to these very left-brained thinkers has had a positive influence on my life. Instead of exclusively using the right side of my brain to make decisions, I learned to also use the left side. Knowing when to use which side—or combining the two—is the key.

Statistics show that many women do not care to concern themselves with money matters (the digital side, left brain or masculine territory). Then they experience a life crisis—a divorce or a death—that forces them to address financial matters. Fortunately I had already learned to use my masculine energy when confronted with the problem of supporting myself into old age. Although I spent most of my adult life as a homemaker, I now have the credentials and experience to be advising you on investment.

It has been said that knowledge is freedom. I certainly feel that way. However you might not. I believe you must never force yourself to do something that wars with your Spirit. If you don't want to learn about investing, find a trusted advisor who will take care of this part of your life. But you would be wise to learn enough to be able to ask the right questions in order to pick out a knowledgeable, trustworthy financial advisor. The important thing is that you begin to take control of your own financial destiny. Winning the lottery or inheriting a huge amount of money are things that do not show up for most of us.

Getting Help—Hiring Experts

If you look ahead at the list of the 10 top reasons for financial failure given at the beginning of Chapter 8, you will come across "Not Knowing What to Do." Don't be afraid to admit that you need help in improving any aspect of your life, particularly your finances. I have always hired experts to complement my abilities. Paying money for "good" advice is smart. Just make certain that the person that you choose to help you with taking charge of your financial life is an expert in the financial field and is honest. When I give financial seminars, I hand out the following sheet on selecting a financial planner or other professional advisor:

When choosing any Professional Advisor, you would be wise to ask the following:

- Number of years of experience? (Be certain that they have not had just one-year's experience repeated over and over again. You want to get the feeling that they have grown professionally.)

- Credentials? (For investment advice, try to work with a Certified Financial Planner.)

- The way they work with regard to:
    - —Fee structure?
    - —Responsibility of each party?
    - —Anticipated time for completion?
    - —Results you can expect?

- What is the firm's specialty?

- Size of the firm?

- Specialists within the firm?

- Why choose her/him over another professional in the same field?

- Do they have references you can call to ask about their work?

Each of us is given certain talents. Perhaps your talent does not include the ability to make good choices for your investments, and you would be wise to seek advice. However, don't sell yourself short. Again, it is the balancing of technical know-how with your intuition that will bring you every kind of success—including financial success.

Setting Long-Term Monetary Goals

In Chapter 1, I promised you a Success Formula for Financial Independence. To achieve control over your financial life, you must "own" this formula. As stated above, it starts with establishing monetary goals. From our earliest lessons in multiplication, we learned that "0" times any number still equals "0." Therefore if we want our money to multiply, we must start to put something aside. The variables you want to initially consider in establishing any wealth-accumulation goals are listed below:

- The amount of money that you need to accumulate (For retirement needs, use the Estimated Retirement Income Worksheet provided later in this chapter),

- The time frame that you are working within (figure at least 20 years of retirement),

- The interest assumptions with regard to the return on your investments (remember to consider your risk tolerance), and

- The inflation rate you assume will be present during your time frame.

These are the basic wealth accumulation elements. Do not feel that you need to be able to supply all of this information right away. Just read through this section of the chapter quickly and come back to it after you have read the entire book.

My objective is to assist you in soon coming up with a realistic dollar amount that you would like to have accumulated for retirement. Whether you see yourself retiring at all is part of your personal vision. However there may come a time when you want to do something else, your company "downsizes," or you cannot work because of poor health. Then the money that you have accumulated has to work for you.

How long do you think that this "retirement nest egg" needs to last? Are you in the age bracket of 36-56? If so, you are known as a "baby boomer." It has been estimated that one out of three of you will live to be over 100. If you are lucky to be at a higher socioeconomic level than the average, you will probably live at least to 100.

In addition to answering the basic questions with regard to amount of money needed, time period, percentage for inflation and return on investment, you would be wise to ask yourself the following:

- At what age do I intend to retire or "slow down?"

- Will I retire completely?

- Will I stay in my present home?

- Do I intend to do a lot of traveling?

- Will Social Security still be viable at the time I'm ready to start receiving benefits?

- How much risk in my investments do I feel comfortable with?

- Keeping in mind my risk tolerance, what return on investment (ROI) can I reasonably assume?

- Does my family have longevity?

Again, don't feel as if you need to know enough now to answer these questions. By the time you finish this book, you will have a solid understanding of what a realistic monetary retirement goal is as well as how some important, basic financial principles will influence your investment success or lack of it. Come back to review this section later and work on these questions then.

For now, I'm going to provide you with some "food for thought" in the form of a chart called "How Long Will My Nest Egg Last?" I often use this chart to drive home the point that one's retirement nest egg has to be quite substantial. You can keep this insight in mind as you use a very practical tool, the Estimated Retirement Income Worksheet, also provided below. This worksheet will help you estimate the amount of money that you will need in retirement.

The assumption in this chart is a starting nest egg of $1,250,000. This money is compounding at an after-tax rate of 8% with a 5% inflation assumption. Naturally the tax would be quite high since the illustrated retiree is taking distributions of $100,000 each year.

While the experts are not predicting an inflation rate as high as 5% for the foreseeable future, the 8% after-tax return would be difficult to obtain in a low-inflation environment. Therefore I've presumed that the percentages will offset one another. You might not have a starting nest egg of over a million dollars, or you may not need $100,000 a

HOW LONG WILL MY NEST EGG LAST?				
YEAR	$100,000 AFTER-TAX STARTING CAPITAL	INCOME ADJUSTED FOR 5% INFLATION	REMAINING CAPITAL	REMAINING CAPITAL INVESTED AT 8% AFTER TAXES
1	$1,250,000	$100,000	$1,150,000	$1,242,000
2	1,242,000	105,000	1,137,000	1,227,960
3	1,227,960	110,250	1,117,710	1,207,127
4	1,207,127	115,763	1,091,364	1,178,673
5	1,178,673	121,551	1,057,122	1,141,692
6	1,141,693	127,628	1,014,064	1,095,189
7	1,095,189	134,010	961,179	1,038,073
8	1,038,073	140,710	897,363	969,152
9	969,152	147,746	821,406	887,119
10	887,119	155,133	731,986	790,544
11	790,544	162,889	627,655	677,868
12	677,686	171,034	506,834	547,381
13	547,381	179,586	367,795	397,218
14	397,218	188,565	208,653	225,345
15	225,345	197,994	27,351	29,539
16	29,439	207,894	BROKE	BROKE

year to live on. If that is the case, simply divide the numbers by 2 or 3. But keep in mind that this chart only covers slightly more than 15 years AND most retirements last longer.

On the next page is the Estimated Retirement Income Worksheet. This will give you a broad idea of what you need to do to prepare for a dignified retirement. It calls for making certain assumptions with regard to the rate of inflation and the rate of return on your investments.

As no one has a crystal ball, these are only "guesstimates." The worksheet is an adaptation taken from a "Personal Financial Planning Guide" published by Newkirk Products, Inc., Albany, New York, a publisher and printer of marketing materials used in the financial service industry.

Many individuals are spending more time in retirement than they did working. The average longevity is 74 years for men and 81 for women. Since that is the average age, which is right in the middle, you have a 50% chance of not reaching that age or living beyond it. Today the fastest growing segment of our society is the 100-year-and-older segment. Be realistic about the amount of money you will need in retirement. In his book, Money Makeovers, Christopher Hayes, Ph.D., says, "Because of their greater longevity, women can least afford to leave their future to chance."

Below I have repeated the questions from above with regard to how you picture your retirement. Yes, I know that the time for this seems a long way off, however it is important that you answer all of these questions soon.

- **At what age do I intend to retire or "slow down?"**
- **Will I retire completely?**
- **Will I stay in my present home?**
- **Do I intend to do a lot of traveling?**
- **Will Social Security still be viable at the time I'm ready to start receiving benefits?**
- **How much investment risk do I feel comfortable with?**
- **Keeping in mind my risk tolerance, what return on investment (ROI) can I reasonably assume?**
- **Does my family have longevity?**

ESTIMATED RETIREMENT INCOME WORKSHEET

	EXAMPLE	YOURS
Current annual income	$40,000	$ _____
Percentage of pre-retirement income needed for retirement	x 80%	x _____
Retirement income needed	$32,000	$ _____
Minus Social Security (The average annual payment in 1998)	($9,180)	($9,180)
Retirement income needed minus Social Security	$22,820	$ _____
Inflation factor (from chart below: example assumes 25 years until retirement)	x 2.67	x _____
Inflation-adjusted retirement income needed	$60,929	_____
Minus projected income from pensions	($5,000)	(_____)
Estimate of annual retirement income needed (In addition to Social Security, pensions, etc.)	$55,929	_____
Savings necessary to produce needed income (Multiply needed income by 15*; example assumes 4% inflation, 7% investment return, and a retirement of 20 years)	$838,935	$ _____
Value of current assets (savings, investments, etc.)	$150,000	$ _____
Growth Factor (from chart below, example assumes 25 years until retirement)	x 3.38	x _____
Estimated future value of current assets	$507,000	$ _____
Total amount you need to save (Subtract the future value of assets from savings necessary to produce needed income; example: $838,935-$507,000)	$331,935	$ _____
Annual amount you need to save (Divide total amount by the investment factor in chart below: example, $331,935 divided by 63.25)	$5,248	$ _____
Monthly amount you need to save (Annual amount divided by 12)	$437	$ _____

*15 is the approximate present value factor for needed income. The actual value factor is 14.877.

Number of years until retirement	5	10	15	20	25	30
Inflation Factor (4% inflation)	1.22	1.48	1.8	2.19	2.67	3.24
Growth Factor (5% return)	1.27	1.62	2.07	2.65	3.38	4.32
Investment Factor (7% return)	5.75	13.82	25.13	41.00	63.25	94.46

Newkirk Products, Inc.

Unleashing Your Analytical Ability & Owning the Success Formula

The Success Formula

$$ + $$

Time +

Good Health +

Low Inflation +

Tax-Favored Environment +

Return on Investment =

Financial Independence

Examining the Reasons Why People Fail Financially

"Ignorance of the Law is no excuse."

JOHN SELDEN, English Jurist and Scholar (1584–1654)

Chapter 8 begins Part III, *Unleashing Your Analytical Ability & Owning the Success Formula,* and this chapter is your opportunity to learn from other people's mistakes. There's a popular saying that states, "Ignorance of the Law is no excuse." After reading this chapter, you will be informed of the top reasons people fail financially. If you identify with one or more of them, you will no longer be able to claim ignorance of the basic "laws" of sound financial planning as your excuse.

The 10 Top Reasons for Financial Failure
1. Ignoring Financial Planning
2. Not Knowing What to Do
3. No Budget
4. Lack of Record-Keeping
5. Not Setting Aside Funds for Investing
6. Poor Cash Flow
7. No Emergency Fund
8. No Debt Management
9. Impulse Buying
10. Being Over or Under Insured

Do any of these describe a particular problem that you are experiencing? If so, the solution is to claim and then "own" the Success

Formula for Financial Independence formally introduced in this part of the book. Let's take a closer look at each of these 10 reasons now.

1. Ignoring Financial Planning

As mentioned earlier, women often avoid planning for their future financial welfare until some life crisis forces them to do this. For many, it seems enough to pay the bills as they come in and to let the future take care of itself. It can even feel as though this is all you can possibly manage, since there is nothing extra left. I often hear of individuals who would like to change their lives, to have some additional spending money for fun. But they seem to be on a treadmill, never getting anywhere. If you are among these people, listen to the message that I'm sending in this book.

Throughout the book, I have been saying that you have the Power to change anything that you want. This includes the power to take charge of your financial future by doing some planning. Again, you are reading this book for a reason. I am assuming that you do want to make some changes in your life. This is a new beginning, and you're right to feel excited! At the same time, you must realize that improving your financial standing is going to require that you do some strategizing and "work."

Perhaps your financial plan will include changing jobs. Great! It's important to dream big, but again you must do the necessary "work." For you, this might mean taking the classes required for changing professions. Note that I have put "work" in quotation marks because as we see our goals being met, we do not view our preparation and action as work. It is simply a means to an end.

2. Not Knowing What to Do

At times, we get stuck. We think that we don't know how to go about changing our lives. That's not true. Within each of us are all of the answers. We simply need to stop and listen, to get in touch with our Inner Voice. Find a quiet place, take some deep breaths, then ask, "What am I supposed to learn?" Then sit still and listen!

After learning what you need to know, do something. Earlier I referred to the tendency most often held by women to analyze a problem to death and then take no action. I termed it "analysis paralysis."

If you have a problem following through on your hunches that come from listening to your Inner Voice, seek out books to help you overcome this tendency. One of the books that helped me is *The Power of Decision* by Raymond Charles Barker. Decision-making is very powerful. Don't deny its usefulness by claiming that you do not know what to do.

3. No Budget

Along with claiming that you don't know what to do is claiming ignorance of where your money went. "Where did all of the money go?" is a frequent question asked at tax time. In order to find out how you are spending your money—including places where you can cut back—use the two monthly cash flow statements below: (1) **Budget: Monthly Income Forecasting** and (2) **Budget: Monthly Expense Forecasting**. But to discover the big picture, you should use the **Annual Cash Flow Statement** (see the next section below). In this way, you can see at a glance how your inflows and outflows match up.

4. Lack of Record-Keeping

Not knowing how you are spending your money causes you to feel out of control. Completing the **Budget: Monthly Income Forecasting** and **Budget: Monthly Expense Forecasting** forms is a must. But at least once a year, you should complete an **Annual Cash Flow Statement.**

Here's a suggestion regarding filling out the Annual Cash Flow Statement. Along the top of a large piece of paper, write all of the expense categories listed on the sample form—plus your individual ones. Then sort out last year's checks under each of the headings. Total the checks in each category and list the amount on your statement. Naturally, for the income portion, you can use your W-2s, 1099s, etc. If you are projecting, you can add any additional income that you expect in the following year.

Another annual form to complete is your **Annual Balance Sheet.** (See the simplified and formal versions on the pages that follow.) This form helps you keep tract of the growth in your assets. It is used to determine your net worth, which is assets minus liabilities. If you are compulsive, you will complete this form every six months, however I recommend doing it once a year.

While you are at it, do not put too much emphasis on the increased equity in your home. It's nice to know, however I classify it differently than other assets. I consider increased home equity to be a "use" asset and not an "investment" asset. To clarify, a "use" asset is one that you do not intend to sell, rather you are using it in your daily life.

Directly below the Annual Balance Sheet, you'll find an insurance section. Your insurance, whether cash value or not, is a part of your estate. Although we are not addressing estate planning, or wealth preservation, in this book, it is wise to be aware of the value of your total estate for estate-tax purposes.

If you are just starting to accumulate financial assets, you might want to use the simplified version of a Balance Sheet that I used with prospects at our first meeting. No matter which of the balance sheets you decide to use, start to keep track of your financial progress.

5. Not Setting Aside Funds for Investing

One of the frequent excuses that I heard from my clients was: "I can't afford to invest." My response was: "Pay yourself first." Somehow we always manage to pay the phone, electric, mortgage payments, etc., therefore we can manage to pay ourselves too.

If you can't discipline yourself enough to invest something on a regular basis, sign up with a mutual fund company. They will arrange for as little as $25 a month to be deducted from your checking account.

If you are convinced that you are better off using "no-load" funds (see Glossary), then call Fidelity, T-Rowe Price, Vanguard, etc. However, if you have found someone (an insurance agent, bank representative or stockbroker) through a recommendation or personal interviewing that you believe and trust, buy the "load fund" from her or him. And remember that it is not what goes in, rather it is what comes out.

You will be surprised at how accustomed you get to not having immediate access to that $25 or whatever amount you initially decide to deduct. Many of you have already found this out by having deductions taken from your paycheck for your 401(k)/403(b). As you become comfortable with the idea of paying yourself first, increase the amount deducted from your checking account. This will be further explored when I focus extensively on mutual funds in Chapter 15, "Structuring Mutual Fund and Stock and Bond Portfolios."

BUDGET: MONTHLY

INCOME SOURCE	JANUARY	FEBRUARY	MARCH	APRIL	MAY
Wages/Salary (you)					
Wages/Salary (spouse)					
(other)					
(other)					
Bonuses					
Moonlighting					
Commissions					
Interest					
Dividends					
Net Rental Inc.					
Annuities					
Pensions					
Social Security					
Other					
Total by Month					

INCOME FORECASTING* Date

JUNE	JULY	AUGUST	SEPTEMBER	OCTOBER	NOVEMBER	DECEMBER

*Note: A three-year supply of the forms on this page and the next
four pages is available free. See order form at back of book.

BUDGET: MONTHLY

	JANUARY	FEBRUARY	MARCH	APRIL	MAY
Fixed Expenses					
IRA					
Savings					
401(k)/403(b)					
Housing					
Telephone					
Gas					
Electric					
Cable					
Loan					
Credit Card					
Car Insurance					
House Insurance					
Life Insurance					
Medical Insurance					
Tax, Federal					
Tax, State					
Tax, FICA					
Tax, Property					
Commuting					
Other					
Variable Expenses					
Food					
Clothing					
Travel					
Entertainment					
Health Club					
Hobbies					
Cleaning					
House Maintenance					
Personal Care					
Medical					
Prescriptions					
Subscriptions					
Education					
Vacation					
Gifts					
Charities					
Spending money					
Car expenses					
New furniture					
Other					
Total by Month					

EXPENSE FORECASTING   Date

JUNE	JULY	AUGUST	SEPTEMBER	OCTOBER	NOVEMBER	DECEMBER

ANNUAL CASH FLOW STATEMENT

Income (You)		Income (Spouse/other)	
Wages/Salary	$	Wages/Salary	$
Bonuses		Bonuses	
Moonlighting		Moonlighting	
Commissions		Commissions	
Interest		Interest	
Dividends		Dividends	
Rental Income		Rental Income	
Pension		Pension	
Annuities		Annuities	
Social Security		Social Security	
Other		Other	
TOTAL	$	TOTAL	$
		TOTAL HOUSEHOLD INCOME	$

Fixed Expenses		Variable Expenses	
IRA		Food	
Savings		Clothing	
401(k)/403/b)		Travel	
Housing		Entertainment	
Telephone		Health Club	
Gas		Hobbies	
Electric		Cleaning	
Cable		House Maintenance	
Loan		Personal Care	
Credit Card		Medical	
Car Insurance		Prescriptions	
House Insurance		Subscriptions	
Life Insurance		Education	
Medical Insurance		Vacation	
Tax, Federal		Gifts	
Tax, State		Charities	
Tax, FICA		Spending money	
Tax, Property		Car expenses	
Commuting		New furniture	
Other		Other	
Other		Other	
Total Fixed Expenses	$	**Total Variable Expenses**	$
		TOTAL EXPENSES	$

ANNUAL BALANCE SHEET

Assets		Liabilities	
Cash (checking/savings)		Mortgage–Residence	
Money Market		Mortgage–Other Real Est.	
CDs (#)		Notes/Accounts Payable	
Stocks (#)		Loans–Banks	
Bonds		Revolving Charge Accts.	
Mutual Funds		Other	
Life Insurance Cash Value			
Notes/Accts. Receivable			
Limited Partnerships (Pub.)			
Limited Partnerships (Priv.)			
Rental Real Estate (#)			
Bus. Interest			
Bus. Interest (Spouse)			
Employee Benefits			
Employee Benefits (Spouse)			
IRA			
IRA (Spouse)			
Keogh			
Keough (Spouse)			
401(k)/403(b)			
401(k)/403(b) (Spouse)			
Residence–Market Val.			
Second Home–Market Val.		**Total Liabilities**	( )
Personal Property			
Total Assets		**Net Worth**	$

Personal Life Insurance

COMPANY & POLICY NO.	AMOUNT	PLAN	DATE	PREMIUM	DIVIDEND	LOANS
Chief Breadwinner	$			$	$	$
	$			$	$	$
	$			$	$	$
Spouse	$			$	$	$
	$			$	$	$
Children	$			$	$	$
	$			$	$	$

SIMPLIFIED VERSION OF BALANCE SHEET

Assets

    Cash and Cash Equivalents

    Checking Accounts

    CDs

    Money Market Accounts

    Credit Union Accounts

    Invested Assets

    Stocks

    Bonds

    Mutual Funds

    401(k) Plans

    403(b) Plans—(These are used

        for non-profit companies.)

    IRAs

      Traditional

      Roth

    Real Estate, other than home

    Use Assets

    Home

    Jewelry

    Automobiles

    Boats

    Other

Total Assets

Liabilities

    Credit Card Debt

    Bank Notes

    Private Loans—From parents, etc

    Mortgage—Home

    Mortgage(s)—Other

Total Liabilities (**)**

Net Worth

Note: This balance sheet can be done on a back of an envelope. The message will be just as clear.

6. Poor Cash Flow

Poor cash flow is related to "Not Setting Aside Funds for Investing"; however, it is somewhat different. You have heard the expression "You can't squeeze blood out of a stone." That might describe your budget. Nevertheless there is a way that you can find the dollars to invest. You CAN improve on your cash flow. Below are some suggestions:

- Trading baby-sitting,

- Swapping skills (e.g., music lessons for foreign language instruction),

- Bartering,

- Mentoring/being mentored, and

- Sharing in the purchase of large-ticket/seldom-used items.

The main idea here is to calculate the amount of money you've saved by using the strategies above and setting those dollars aside for investing. These amounts will add up quickly.

Trading baby-sitting not only saves you money that you can then invest, it also provides peace of mind. I tend to be serious about everything that I do. This included motherhood. Within our neighborhood, we had four couples who shared not only baby-sitting but bridge. We kept a tally of the baby-sitting hours that each couple contributed. When my husband and I went out for an evening of fun, how pleasurable it was to know that there was an adult to deal with anything unexpected—like one of the children waking up with a severe earache, etc. In addition, some of us also played bridge once a month. This was pleasant and supplied a very cheap form of entertainment. The dollars saved on movie tickets, etc., can also be diverted into an investment fund.

Swapping skills/talents/knowledge is another way to avoid spending money that you can invest. Examine your life to find out what would be of value to someone else, then post your swapping proposal on bulletin boards in your area. Don't give up; let your subconscious suggest places. I was trained to teach Spanish, so I arranged to swap Spanish lessons for those in German. The other person and I both benefited.

Bartering involves swapping actual goods instead of talents and knowledge. Bartering is a way of life for many. Again, both parties benefit and investment dollars can be found.

Mentoring and being mentored can supply investment money by saving the cost of classes, seminars, books, etc. Also, there are other advantages. When we mentor, we give of ourselves, our energy. And since it is easier for most of us to give than to receive, we feel good when we mentor. But, as always, balance is best. To profit the most, we would be wise not to only mentor but to be mentored. By forming a relationship with individuals who have experience in one of the areas that we lack, we expand our consciousness, which really is our intelligence.

Sharing in the purchase of large-ticket/seldom-used items is yet another way to create investment dollars. Consider purchasing these with someone else or even renting them together. Examples of this might include a snow blower, a leaf blower/vacuum, a summer home or even a yacht. Before my brother accumulated his wealth, he jointly owned a 44-foot sailboat with three other couples. They had a schedule for when each pair was entitled to use the boat. My friend Linda owns a month in a home at Hilton Head Island. Several of my children, as well as my clients, own time-shares. Their use offers great savings as well as enjoyment.

7. No Emergency Fund

Not having a cash reserve for emergencies and/or long-term investment causes a negative feeling of insecurity. The wolf is always at your door. It is very difficult to project confidence when worrying about lack of money.

I have already related that at the time of my second divorce, my emergency fund allowed me to move back to my hometown. It also gave me the time to seek employment in a new industry. Coming as I did from the search and recruitment field, I knew how to go about seeking a job. But since I was changing industries, this naturally took a little longer. As already stated, worrying and focusing on lack and limitation brings it into our lives. Had I not had the emergency fund, I could not have projected the necessary self-confidence.

Paying credit-card interest, which is not tax-deductible, while sitting on large amounts of money in low-yielding and taxable bank accounts is poor planning. However good planning DOES include having an emergency fund in what we, in the financial world, term "cash equivalents" (savings accounts, interest-bearing checking accounts, money market funds, CDs, etc.). This emergency fund should equal the money that would be needed to pay your fixed expenses for at least three to six months should you become ill or unemployed.

Cashing in a CD before its maturity date would cause a penalty, but there's another way to use these funds. If you need to find money for an emergency, you can obtain a loan against the principal in the CD. You will be charged a couple of percentage points over what your CD is earning, however the net cost is much cheaper than suffering the economic loss from having to pay a penalty for early surrender. Bank accounts and CDs can be backed up with a tax-exempt bond fund, which will be discussed in a later chapter, Chapter 15, "Structuring Mutual Fund/Stock and Bond Portfolios."

8. No Debt Management

Wise management of debt is another tool to use in bettering your financial position. Often we have had it drilled into us that paying cash is "good" while charging anything is "bad." However the wise use of credit is definitely positive. Reverse your thinking.

When you are considering buying, for example, a new automobile, establish a line of credit against the built-up equity in your home. This is known as a Home Equity Line of Credit or a HELC. You will not pay any interest for the credit line until you use it. Also, the interest not only is reasonable, it is also tax-deductible. However, for this method to be effective, you must commit to paying back the loan over a certain period of time, say five years. Remember, this is short-term debt; a new car will wear out long before 30 years.

Even if you don't already own a home, taking out a regular loan and making payments establishes your credit. The important thing is that the loan you make does not carry a high interest rate, e.g. credit-card interest. People who have paid cash for everything are often denied mortgages. They have never established a credit history. Here is where our third "d" comes in. You must discipline yourself to pay back the loan in a timely manner.

You probably have heard the expression "using other people's money." This is what leveraging and wise debt management is all about. I am not suggesting that you take on a lot of debt. What I am suggesting is that you find a way not to pull down from invested capital. By invested capital, we mean money put aside to grow into a sizable amount for a later need. By not touching the investments that you already have in place, your investments will compound. Through the "miracle of compounding," you will be able to accumulate the money you'll need for your long-term money goals. (The subject of compounding will be thoroughly explored in the next chapter, "Recognizing the Time Value of Money.")

Another way to use debt to your advantage is to take out a 30-year mortgage rather than a 15-year mortgage. This is especially true if the individual or couple is in a high tax bracket. The difference in the amount of payment between the 15-year and the 30-year mortgage can be invested in a tax-exempt bond fund. If the individual or couple has a psychological need to be mortgage free within 15 years, the bond fund can pay off the mortgage.

9. Impulse Buying

One habit among people who are poor money managers is buying items on impulse. Before you buy a "bargain," ask yourself, "If this wasn't on sale, would I buy it?" Oftentimes the answer is "no." I always brought my "bargains" to Manhattan for my wardrobe consultant, Irene, to approve. Invariably she would ask, "Do you really love it?" This is an excellent question to ask yourself before buying/keeping a "bargain."

Usually we discover that the things that we thought were cheap, we don't love or need. Always look for value. With practice, you will intuitively know when something shows up in your life that you should buy. You will learn to trust that the thought to buy this item and the very appearance of it is not a coincidence. When the Spirit speaks to you, act. I have found that even if I don't think that I need something at the time I'm inspired to buy it, eventually the item is exactly what I needed or wanted.

In addition, the improper use of credit cards can contribute to buying items that you do not need. This can become a vicious cycle. At times, all that you can afford to do is pay off the credit card interest, thereby you never reduce the principal. If credit card debt is one of your money problems, you probably would be wise to only use cash and to pay down the entire credit card debt as soon as possible.

10. Being Over or Under Insured

Another possible leakage in your cash flow could come from being over or under insured. One should examine each of the risks that might be covered by insurance, determine if the risk is large compared to the premium, and then act accordingly. In other words, you should only insure for catastrophic risks.

No matter what kind of insurance it is, I view it as a method of leveraging your dollars. Remember, leveraging means using other people's money. With insurance, you are paying relatively small premiums to protect a potentially large financial loss.

For example, while a couple is raising their children, I strongly recommend the purchase of term insurance on the breadwinner as well as on the caregiver (who is usually the wife). Should one of the parents die before the children have finished college, the insurance proceeds would provide financial assistance. In addition, since husbands usually die before their wives, it is important that enough assets are available to pay for her living expenses. Insurance is a good source of creating some or all of the necessary assets.

I am a firm believer in insurance as an economic tool to be used in all financial planning. However, in my opinion, certain types of insurance are not good tools. An example is indemnity insurance. Indemnity insurance is used for a specific risk. For instance, the big "C" or cancer causes many people to panic and purchase cancer protection policies. While a policy won't protect the buyer from getting cancer, it could give her or him peace of mind.

I once had a client who had witnessed the high cost of taking care of a cancer patient. He had no less than five policies covering cancer. At the same time, he not only had Medicare but a very good major medical plan. All of this cancer insurance was not needed. If my memory serves me correctly, the premiums of these excess policies were costing about $8,000 a year. It took a little convincing, however my client finally realized that he was paying for a coverage that he would never use.

Another example of a policy that probably will never be used is a hospital indemnity policy. Again, this policy covers a specific thing, providing money for lengthy stays in the hospital. For instance, the terms might state that the policyholder is guaranteed the money to pay for a 60-day hospital stay. However, the reality is that the government limits hospital stays.

Here, in the US, we have what are known as Medical Directives or DRGs. The government put these in place because the cost of long hospital stays for individuals was constantly escalating each year, especially for people on Medicare. But these directives limit the amount of days for each type of sickness for everyone. Recently the courts have ruled that the two-day stay directive for mothers giving birth was inadequate. So the directives have been controversial.

Other Reasons for Financial Failure

In the remaining chapters of this book, I will be discussing additional reasons why people fail financially. Here are five more reasons that will be addressed:

Five More Reasons for Financial Failure
1. Procrastination
2. Lack of Feel for Investing
3. Failure to Understand Tax Laws
4. Not Including Inflation into One's Calculations
5. Not Diversifying Investments

These reasons, among others, will be interspersed in material covering my Success Formula as well as certain investment basics. Want to learn how to invest intelligently? Want to make your financial future more secure? Keep reading.

- Do you relate to any of the cited reasons for financial failure?

- Do you now have a better idea of how to budget and keep financial records?

- Are you paying yourself first?

- Did you find some cash to invest?

- Do you better understand the use of debt as a means of improving your finances?

- Are you taking full advantage of the benefits of saving in your company's savings plan?

- Are you under or over insured?

CHAPTER

9

Recognizing the Time Value of Money

"Women start saving later and save less than men."

BUREAU OF LABOR STATISTICS

With this chapter, we will begin to look at the more technical financial information related to investing. Hopefully my gift to you is to be able to explain these somewhat complicated principles in a simple manner. Remember the old cliché, "Rome wasn't built in a day!" Your ability to comfortably work with financial concepts will also not come in a day.

Here again is the foolproof "Success Formula for Financial Independence" that I developed very early in my career as a financial consultant. I have used it in the countless seminars that I have given:

SUCCESS FORMULA:

$$
\begin{array}{c}
\$\$ \\
+ \\
\text{TIME} \\
+ \\
\text{GOOD HEALTH} \\
+ \\
\text{LOW INFLATION} \\
+ \\
\text{TAX-FAVORED ENVIRONMENT} \\
+ \\
\text{RETURN ON INVESTMENT} \\
= \\
\textbf{FINANCIAL INDEPENDENCE}
\end{array}
$$

I guarantee that if you fully grasp—i.e. "own"—the concepts within this formula, you will be financially successful.

As previously pointed out, we are concerned with having a large enough retirement nest egg when we need and want one. To do that, we must have a long-range financial plan. The money used in our plan has to grow into a sizable amount. To make this happen, we must start to accumulate the necessary money. Although we must start with an amount of money, continually add to it, and leave it in place, it is not the amount of money that matters most—it is the *length of time* that it is invested.

Procrastination

The number one reason for not providing for a dignified retirement is not getting started in time or procrastination. It is only through ridding ourselves of what I term "stinkin' thinkin'" that we can end this bad habit. Yet simply forcing ourselves to take any action is only a temporary solution. If you determine that procrastination is a trait that you presently have, it might be wise to use the chart "Make Your Choice Positive," featuring positive and negative character traits selected by Jack Boland, which I have included in Chapter 3. While you are looking at the chart, you might also look for some related bad habits that you need to change.

In our daily lives, procrastination shows up as dependence, worry and indecisiveness. The cure is action, making decisions. Because we are stepping out of our "familiar" zone, this might cause some discomfort. The consequence of not eradicating false beliefs that cause defeating behavior is failure. The illustration on the next page will graphically send home the message of why it is so important to DO IT NOW!

From this example, the unsophisticated reader might question that one person invested a total of *$14,000* over a 7-year period while the other person invested *$62,000* over a 31-year period, and yet the person who invested *$48,000 less* actually has more accumulated at age 65. This illustrates the chapter title, "Recognizing the Time Value of Money."

The Rule of 72

The Rule of 72 is a very good rule to know. With it, you can quickly figure out how long it will take for your money to double. Divide the number 72 by your expected rate of return on your investment.

$$$ PROCRASTINATION COSTS $$$

	At age 28, an individual starts investing $2,000 annually at 10% for 7 years		At age 35, an individual starts investing $2,000 annually at 10% for 31 years	
AGE	**ANNUAL CONTRIBUTION**	**ACCUMULATED CONTRIBUTIONS**	**ANNUAL CONTRIBUTION**	**ACCUMULATED CONTRIBUTIONS**
28	$2,000	$2,000	$0	
29	2,000	4,000	0	
30	2,000	6,000	0	
31	2,000	8,000	0	
32	2,000	10,000	0	
33	2,000	12,000	0	
34	2,000	$14,000	0	
35	0		$2,000	$2,000
36	0		2,000	4,000
37	0		2,000	6,000
38	0		2,000	8,000
39	0		2,000	10,000
40	0		2,000	12,000
41	0		2,000	14,000
42	0		2,000	16,000
43	0		2,000	18,000
44	0		2,000	20,000
45	0		2,000	22,000
46	0		2,000	24,000
47	0		2,000	26,000
48	0		2,000	28,000
49	0		2,000	30,000
50	0		2,000	32,000
51	0		2,000	34,000
52	0		2,000	36,000
53	0		2,000	38,000
54	0		2,000	40,000
55	0		2,000	42,000
56	0		2,000	44,000
57	0		2,000	46,000
58	0		2,000	48,000
59	0		2,000	50,000
60	0		2,000	52,000
61	0		2,000	54,000
62	0		2,000	56,000
63	0		2,000	58,000
64	0		2,000	60,000
65	0		2,000	$62,000
	Total including compounded interest at age 65 $331,085		**Total including compounded interest at age 65 $328,988**	

Example 1: **Assumption: Investment return of 10%**
Divide 72 by 10. By doing this, you learn that it will take 7.2 years for your original investment to double in value.

Example 2: **Assumption: Bank-type return of 3%**
Divide 72 by 3. By doing this, you learn that it will take 24 years for your original investment to double in value.

Now you can see the value of not placing your savings in low-yielding investments. Later you will see that it is the net return that you must consider. To get at this figure (the net amount), you must also include the impact that inflation and taxes have on your return.

The Miracle of Compounding

Albert Einstein said, "Compounding is the greatest invention of modern times." Along with the Rule of 72, an understanding of the "Miracle of Compounding" is vital to successful investing. This is how the "miracle" looks:

Example: **Assumptions: One-time investment of $10,000, 10% return**

Year	1st	5th	10th	15th	20th
% Earned	10%	12.5%	17.0%	22.5%	28.6%
Value	$10,000	$16,105	$25,937	$41,772	$67,275

The money must stay invested during the entire time illustrated. It is not "revolving-door" money. As you can see, this example is really quite dramatic. Even though the investment's return is stated to be 10% annually, by allowing the investment to compound, the investment's return is much, much higher.

This is the miracle. The reason that the investment grows so rapidly is that it's not only the principal—the original $10,000—that is earning interest. In addition, the interest on the principal is also earning interest.

While it is easier to understand how compounding works when we use a fixed-income (fixed-interest) type investment, compounding also

HOW COMPOUNDING WORKS

YEAR	INVESTMENT	INTEREST RATE	INTEREST EARNED	TOTAL VALUE
1	$10,000	10%	$1,000	$11,000
2	0	10%	1,100	12,100
3	0	10%	1,210	13,310
4	0	10%	1,331	13,641
5	0	10%	1,464	16,105
6	0	10%	1,611	17,716
7	0	10%	1,772	19,487
8	0	10%	1,949	21,436
9	0	10%	2,144	23,579
10	0	10%	2,358	25,937
11	0	10%	2,594	28,531
12	0	10%	2,853	31,384
13	0	10%	3,138	34,523
14	0	10%	3,452	37,975
15	0	10%	3,797	41,772
16	0	10%	4,177	45,950
17	0	10%	4,595	50,545
18	0	10%	5,054	55,599
19	0	10%	5,560	61,159
20	0	10%	6,116	67,275

takes place in variable (read stock) type investments. If the investment had been in the stock market in recent years, it would have grown to a larger number. However you would have had to weather the storm of 1994 when practically every asset class had a negative return.

Since the market does fluctuate—causing the investor's return to fluctuate with regard to appreciation—compounding is a little more difficult to understand with a stock type investment. But some stocks, not all, pay regular dividends. This dividend amount—added to the average appreciation over a long period—can be used to determine your return.

Be certain to learn the concepts of the Rule of 72 and the Miracle of Compounding. They come in quite handy.

The Cost of Waiting

In an early section of this chapter, "Procrastination," you saw a graphic example of how time affects the accumulation of a capital fund. Now let's look at the same concept in the form of a $2,000 IRA contribution.

Example:	Assumptions: $2,000 invested annually at 8% to age 65			
Age Started	25	35	45	55
No. of Years	40 yrs	30 yrs	20 yrs	10yrs
Amount	$518,113	$226,566	$91,524	$28,973

Once again, you can see how important it is to get started. Take an individual who is 65 years old. The person has just been laid off from a job and seeks advice from a financial planner. The individual estimates that 70% of her/his pre-retirement income of $30,000 would be sufficient to meet living expenses. That means that she/he must earn $21,000 ($30,000 x .70 = $21,000) each year.

Having only started to think about retirement 10 years earlier at age 55, and being able to set aside just $2,000 a year, we see that the retirement fund is $28,973. It is quite obvious without even working the numbers that this individual cannot retire. Even if the retiree were able to supplement the Social Security income by working, she/he would have to give back $1.00 of Social Security income for every $3.00 earned above $15,500. In fact, if this person were only 62, she/he would have to give back $1.00 for every $2.00 over $9,600. These numbers are indexed, i.e., tied to the Consumer Price Index (CPI), which is a measure of inflation. As it is now, earned income in excess of the Social Security limits is taxed until age 70. Also, keep in mind that people born after 1959 are not eligible for any Social Security until age 67.

Impatience

Impatience is an additional reason why people fail financially, one that I did not mention earlier. It is a matter of statistics that the average investor does exactly the opposite of what should be done to accumulate money. Too often they buy when the market is going up and sell when the market is going down. The movement in the market often prompts the investor's response. However investing is not like shooting craps. Seldom are there quick profits. For the miracle of compounding to happen, the investor must adopt a non-trader personality and stay in the market for the long haul.

Below is a chart based on research done by the independent marketing group, Dalbar.

INDIVIDUAL INVESTOR PERFORMANCE

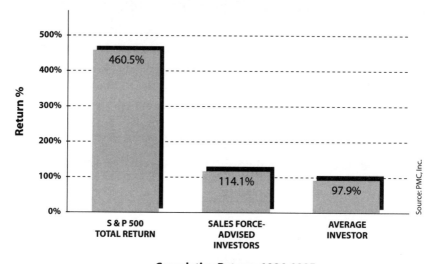

Based on recent research, individual investors making use of market timing do not do as well as typical market averages.

Cumulative Returns 1984-1995

From the chart above, the reader might ask: "Why not simply buy an S&P Index fund?" Read my article in Chapter 13, "The Capital Markets 1996." As long as the fundamentals—earnings, industry position, amount of debt, etc.—of a company are OK, the investor would be wise to ignore market sentiment. In fact, the old adage to "buy on bad news" has proven correct over a period of time. A smart investment move is to buy the shares that others are undervaluing and hold onto them through all of the market cycles—i.e., the ups and downs of the stock and bond markets.

Later in the book, I will mention my holding in Analog Devices, Inc. I will relate how I bought this stock in 1979, buying 100 shares at $21. Believing that the stock was "undervalued" when its price went down to $15.75 a few months later, I bought another 100 shares. This is "averaging down." My share price became $18.375 (100 shares @ $21 = $2,100; add 100 shares @ $15.75 = $1,575 for a total of $3,675 divided by 200). During the 1980s, small cap stocks, like Analog Devices, were out of favor. However I believed in the fundamentals of the company and held onto my stock. Unfortunately I did not buy more. But even with that seeming mistake, my holding today is worth in the area of $90,000. This is an example of buying a stock that is undervalued and being patient.

Two predominate traits of women are patience and not acting impulsively. This bodes well for good investing. However another trait that women seem to have in abundance is being passive. Women have to learn when to be patient and when to take action. Women can easily learn to make this determination by listening to their intuition, being their own authority, and not relying on other people's advice. Unfortunately, as it now stands, according to Hayes, girls develop "clipped wings" after adolescence. What he means is that they give up their own authority and rely on the opinion of others regarding what is good for them.

Being one's own authority often takes courage. It means going against the herd mentality. The correct thing to do is to buy the stocks that you have researched, hold them no matter what the market does, and if possible buy more. Continuously putting money into the market is called "dollar cost averaging." This is the very best way to invest as will be explained more fully in Chapter 13, "Understanding Return on Investment." Again, don't pay attention to what's happening in the market over a few days, months or years. Successful investors use a very long time frame.

And women need to be counted among the successful investors, because:

1. Between one-third and two-thirds of women now aged thirty-five to fifty-five will be impoverished after age sixty-five if they do not immediately start to prepare financially for their later years. (Source: National Center for Women and Retirement Research, NCWRR)

2. Most single women will have only one-third to one-fifth of the money they'll need to retire comfortably. (Source: OppenheimerFunds, Inc.)

3. Only 40% of women have company-sponsored pension plans. They are only half as likely to work for companies that provide them. (Source: Department of Labor)

4. Women invest more conservatively. 75% of women have their savings in bank-type investments. (Source: NCWRR)

5. Female households now represent 18% of those in the US. (Source: US Census Bureau)

6. Almost half of all marriages end in divorce. (Source: National Center for Health Statistics)

7. The average age of widowhood is 56. (Source: US Census Bureau)

8. 52% of elderly women live alone. (Source: US Census Bureau)

9. The proportion of women who had never married tripled from 1970 to 1994, from 6% to 20%. (Source: US Census Bureau)

10. Women on average outlive their spouses by seven years. (Source: US Census Bureau)

11. Women earn 72% of their male counterparts' earnings. (Source: US Census Bureau, 1995).

12. Women aged 15 and over who worked year-round, full-time in 1993 earned a median of $21,747. (Source: US Census Bureau)

13. In 1930, women had 3.4 years of retirement; 1960, 8.1 years; 1990, 13.8 years. (Source: US Census Bureau)

14. 80% to 90% of all women will be responsible for their own finances at some point. (Source: US Census Bureau)

One woman who transformed herself from a "financial ignoramus" into a savvy investor is Gina Garrubbo. In the September 21, 1998 issue of *Forbes,* she was featured in an article entitled, "Women Are from Venus and Men Are from Wall Street" by Ann Marsh. Ms. Garrubbo is Executive VP of the second largest Web site targeted to women, women.com, with 30 million page views a month.

The author says, "THEN: Married at 28, Garrubbo says she was $8,000 in credit card debt, even though she was making in the low six figures in a national television sales job. Her husband minded the assets while she worked and spent" Ms. Marsh quotes Garrubbo as saying, "I wasn't focused on finance." The writer continues, "NOW: Garrubbo picks her own stock and is diversified into real estate. . . ."

Just to review, we have examined Procrastination, the Rule of 72, the Miracle of Compounding, the Cost of Waiting, and Impatience. These concepts are important for women to grasp. Work with them until you "own" them. Examine your own style of investing. Think about the concept of procrastination. Have you started to set aside a portion of your earnings in order to build a retirement nest egg? Did the chart "Procrastination Costs" send a message? Do you understand why "time is of the essence?"

Does the use of the Rule of 72 indicate that you need to take more risk, i.e. obtain a better return on your investments? Are you allowing your money to stay in investments in order to compound? How old are you? Can you relate to the story about the person who started their retirement savings too late? Finally, are you using your wonderful gift of patience in your investing?

Just to make certain that you have the message of this chapter, here are some additional questions:

- **Have you started saving for your retirement?**

- **Is the Rule of 72 new to you? If so, look for ways to practice using this rule to determine how long it will take for your money to double with a particular type of investment.**

- **Do you grasp the importance of leaving your money in an investment so it will compound?**

- **Did the illustrations alert you to the cost of waiting to start investing?**

- **Do you go with the herd with regard to buying when the market is going up, and selling when the market is going lower?**

- **Do you recognize that you might be counted in one of the above statistics?**

- **Do you identify with Gina Garrubbo's former credit card debt?**

Pursuing Perfect Health

"80% of widows now living in poverty were not poor
before the death of their husband."

US DEPARTMENT OF COMMERCE

People sometimes ask, "Why do you include good health in your formula for Financial Independence?" My answer is simple. Unless we are able to work, we won't be able to accumulate the necessary dollars for retirement. Also, today men die earlier than women. The average age of widowhood is 56. This means that quite often women become impoverished when they become widows.

Statistics published by the US Census Bureau in a statistical brief dated September, 1995, state that: "More Women These Days Live Alone." Fifty-two percent of women ages 75 or older live alone; 31% of those aged 65-74 do. These statistics should send home a poignant message. Also, it is good to keep in mind that 50% of the husband's pension usually dies with him. Also, the survivor, usually the wife, receives only one Social Security check—the larger of the two (hers or his).

From my experience, it is often difficult to demand that our husbands practice good health habits. This means that we must stay healthy and become financially independent so we do not wind up with too few assets to live comfortably. It might be wise for wives to insist that their husbands—who are usually providing the bulk of the household income—be adequately insured with life insurance. Should the husband die prematurely, the insurance proceeds, which are received tax-free, can provide the necessary income stream for the widow.

Loss of income with the accompanying loss of assets is common from death; however, loss of income from a long-term disability is even more common. Men as a group currently experience a higher rate of disability. Statistics from the US Department of Health & Human Services state that "from age 20 to age 60, men have a 19% chance of acquiring a disability (an illness that will last more than 90 days); women have a 15% chance." In fact, the government reported in its 1981 population survey that 8.5% of all working-age women in the US were disabled. And, the highest incidence of disability in women of working age is in the age group of 45-54.

In addition to these statistics, information from the Society of Actuaries shows the following with regard to the average length of a long-term disability:

HOW LONG DOES THE AVERAGE LONG-TERM DISABILITY LAST?			
Age	30	40	50
Length of Disability	3 yrs.	5.5 yrs.	6.2 yrs.

Disability Health Insurance

The above statistics would indicate that you might be wise to purchase disability health insurance to protect your income stream. This is a classic example of the economic use of insurance. Disability is a catastrophic risk, presenting a large potential loss. If you doubt this, take out a calculator and determine your potential income stream until age 65. As a percentage of the loss, the premium is small. As I recommended earlier, this is the correct use of insurance: allowing a relatively small amount of money to protect against a possibly enormous loss.

Most of us insure our automobiles, homes and health. These are also potentially large losses, however the probability of suffering these types of losses is actually much lower than that for a long-term disability. Below is a probability study:

PROBABILITY OF SUFFERING A LOSS ON CERTAIN ASSETS			
Asset	Automobile	Home	Health	Disability
Loss probability	1/70	1/88	1/105	1/8

These statistics might be hard to believe, however think of a time when you heard of someone having a car accident or that her or his home burnt down. It doesn't happen that often. And although it would seem that people are going into the hospitals on a daily basis, the odds for any one person are fairly remote overall. Note that the statistic under "Health" is one for the number of times that people use their health insurance to pay for catastrophic healthcare costs.

Not too many years ago, insuring our stream of income through the purchase of long-term disability insurance was comparatively easy. In fact, there were policies that protected your income stream in your own occupation up until age 65. In other words, you could take another job and still collect benefits. However recently the disability insurance industry has suffered horrendous losses. Therefore it is much more difficult to obtain personal disability insurance, and the benefits have been substantially reduced.

While many of the larger corporations continue to insure their employees against long-term disability in the form of a group policy, these policies do not compare to the individual policies that were available in the past. Often these policies are tied to one's being able to qualify for disability under Social Security, which is quite difficult to do. In addition, the amount of benefit is often offset by any payments received from the state, Social Security, etc. This amount is further reduced by taxes.

Furthermore, unlike the "your occupation" policies explained above, these group policies usually require "total disability"—i.e., you will not receive any payments if you are able to work at any occupation. If the individual takes a job just to keep busy, she/he loses all benefits. Many individuals have already experienced the reduction in lifestyle due to the "downsizing" of large corporations. Added to the distress of being laid off is the fact that many middle managers and others were left without the protection of long-term disability insurance. Being "downsized" might cause a reduction in lifestyle; suffering a long-term disability certainly does.

As this book is concerned with "wealth accumulation," and not "wealth protection," we will only briefly cover the important subject of protecting assets through the purchase of long-term care insurance. In my opinion, long-term care insurance can be used effectively to protect estates valued between one-third and two-thirds of a million dollars, i.e., around $350,000 to $700,000. If the estate is smaller, there usually are not enough assets to cover the premiums on long-term care insurance. In estates closer to one million dollars, there probably will be enough assets to cover caring for someone to old age. Again, in my opinion, the best time to purchase long-term care insurance is while one is in the early to late sixties and is still healthy. Naturally, the contract must have a good inflation clause. Here, again, do your research.

Healthy Lifestyle

The important thing is to stay healthy. If you are unable to or do not choose to purchase long-term disability insurance, you can protect your health by choosing a healthy lifestyle. Studies indicate that eating properly is very important to good health. Today people tend to be more health conscious than in the past, and they are including more vegetables and fruit in their diets. Yet one out of three adults in the US is considered obese—at least 20 pounds over their ideal weight. And the statistics for our youth are even more frightening.

Hopefully these statistics will change soon. I am one who still believes in the old adage, "You are what you eat." By including all the basic food groups in our daily food plan, we keep our bodies balanced. To stay in sync or healthy, we need to be eating properly. If we are experiencing illness, we need to seek advice on what is lacking in our diet. A qualified nutritionist can evaluate our eating habits and even perform tests to determine what our bodies are lacking.

Alternative medicine can also be used to maintain our health. Chinese acupuncture and Japanese massage are two possibilities. These healing arts are many centuries old. It is only recently that the industrial world has recognized their usefulness. By combining Western medicine with the Eastern healing arts, we can stay healthy and keep our bodies in a balanced state.

In addition to eating well and utilizing both Western and Eastern medicine, exercising is important. I have been active all of my life. As a mother of six children, I did not have to plan extra ways to exercise. After the children had grown, I started exercising regularly—first at Jazzercise and later at health clubs. In addition, the 12 years with my long-term boyfriend Rich included countless bike and ski trips.

I still ski and bike, however not as much. During the spring, summer and fall, I play tennis twice a week at the nearby Grant Park. During the winter, I try to exercise three times a week in the health club. And because I no longer have or need a car in downtown Chicago, I take public transportation and walk everywhere.

All of this has paid off. While living in New Jersey, I took part in a study conducted by one of the doctors who attended my financial seminars at the School of Medicine and Dentistry in Newark, New Jersey. It was a study of the immune systems in people over age 60. When my test results came back, the nurse was astounded at the results. "I have never seen such a healthy immune system in a women of any age. Yours is better than the young man assisting me." More recently, I had my bone density checked. I was above average in all categories in spite of the fact that I do not take hormones. I am rarely sick and am blessed with continuous high energy.

Meditation

Another method that I use to maintain perfect health is meditation, which is simply a method of quieting our thoughts. In over 400 studies, the health of participants was shown to improve when they meditated for 20 minutes twice a day. Maharishi Mahesh Yogi, in his book *Science of Being and Art of Living—Transcendental Meditation,* states that the practice of meditation will bring lower stress and anxiety as well as improve physical and mental health. He also reports that reductions of 50% or more in health care costs have been observed in all age groups.

Currently I make a conscious effort to meditate. However many years ago, as a young mother of five children under five years of age, I intuitively meditated. Here is the story.

Exactly at 12:50 in the afternoon, I would set the timer on my Caloric stove for 10 minutes. I insisted that each of the children be quiet—the younger ones napped, the older ones read, and none of them dared to call to me or otherwise bother me during those precious 10 minutes. All of the neighbors—including the children—knew of my daily practice.

I would curl up on the living room couch in a fetal position, covering myself with an old, green, moth-eaten wool cardigan. Then I'd sandwich my head between two sofa pillows and instruct my mind to close out all thoughts. Remarkably, these 10 minutes were sufficient to renew my energy. I could then continue my hectic life until 9:30 or 10:00 at night. And since my young husband was absent from the home each workday (plus putting in two evenings a week and all day Saturday at his second job), I needed this energy to attend to our children. It was not until recently that I recognized that I was not just resting, I was meditating!

Try this. One common way to meditate is to focus your attention on a sound called a mantra and to let go of all thoughts. The following meditation exercise uses the commonly used mantra "Om."

1. Sit in a comfortable chair or lie down on the couch or bed. Close your eyes.

2. Relax as you slowly breathe in and out several times.

3. Repeat the mantra "Om" silently and slowly in your mind. If a thought interrupts this process, notice it, and then bring your attention back to the mantra. Let a soothing rhythm develop as you repeat the mantra slowly over and over again.

4. Allow yourself to sink deeper and deeper into your Inner Self. Continue to relax as you repeat the mantra. Notice any thoughts that come into your mind and then let them go.

5. Stay with the meditation for 10 to 20 minutes. It is not unusual to receive flashes of insight during this time. Solutions to problems often come during meditation. Receive the insight and then go back to repeating the mantra.

6. At the end of the meditation, open your eyes. Give yourself a few more moments of quiet and relaxation before you return refreshed to your day.

There are many ways to meditate, and the above exercise is very basic. See the Glossary for books that offer additional ideas.

Oneness with Nature

Besides meditation, identifying with our oneness with Nature, as mentioned earlier, has positive benefits. Again, we are drawn to things and persons who reinforce our beliefs. I have always been an admirer of American architect Frank Lloyd Wright, who was a lover of Nature. Wright believed a building's form should be strongly influenced by its natural environment. Few people realize how "otherworldly" Wright was. Recently while watching a rerun of a 1950s interview of Wright by a young Mike Wallace, I heard the architect say, "I spell God with a capital 'N.'" In other words, he viewed Nature as God. What is your relationship with Nature?

Staying close to Nature will teach us to give up struggle, to be joyful and thankful. This *joie de vivre* comes when we accept whatever shows up in our lives. I was previously aware of the wonderful prayer asking God to help me to fully accept whatever I could not change and to grant me the wisdom to differentiate between my responsibility and God's, but I seldom used it. Had I been wiser, I would have. Today my favorite expression is, "Divine Right Action is taking place right now."

Making Wise Health Care Decisions

Fortunately people in the US are beginning to take more responsibility for their own health. Heretofore we have treated physicians as though they were gods, never questioning what we were told. Not only are individuals taking more responsibility, they are seeking out alternative methods of healing. In fact, many insurance companies have begun paying for these types of healing.

A personal story might help you to understand that, as stated over and over again, you have all of the answers within you.

About 13 years ago, I had been experiencing pain in my lower left leg. This pain first showed up when I lived in Downers Grove, Illinois. My family doctor thought that I had a sports injury since I was doing quite a bit of aerobics at the time. I stated that it was not; I simply woke one morning with the pain.

Not to go into this too deeply but to make the point, suffice it to say that I went to an orthopedic doctor and he did all kinds of treatments. None of them helped. After moving to New Jersey, I sought out an internist. He prescribed muscle relaxants. Again, no improvement. Then I went to another orthopedist. He put me through all sorts of diagnostic tests, including a test for nerve damage. When he suggested that maybe it would be of benefit if I had both legs—not just the one that was affected—put in casts, I knew that it was time to move on.

I consulted another internist. And although the pain I was experiencing could be read in my eyes, he told me to *"Go home and forget about it."* He added, *"After all, you are able to function."* It was at this time that I mentioned my dilemma to Reverend Gwen Gillespie, the Minister at the Princeton Science of the Mind Church. She asked me if I was meditating on the problem. I responded that I just didn't have time. She stated, *"Well, you won't get better until you do."*

128

So wanting to get better, I started to meditate. On the second day of these very abbreviated meditation sessions, my arches started to burn. It was then that I remembered that all during my childbearing years, I had worn oxfords with arch supports in them. But now that I no longer was "just a housewife" but a career woman, I dressed for the office; this meant wearing high-heeled shoes. Could it be that I needed arch supports?

Through a suggestion from the General Agent's secretary, I went to see a podiatrist. He asked me to walk so that he could examine my gait. I felt ridiculous since I could hardly walk because of the severe pain. After watching me, he stated, *"You are walking all wrong.* The pain that you are feeling is caused by the muscle that is pressing on a nerve."

He made casts of my feet and from there he constructed arch supports or orthotics, which were leather insoles with bits of plastic pasted on the bottom. These devices allowed me to walk correctly. Wonder of wonders, after going through four years of my life in pain, the minute that I started walking on those arch supports, the pain was gone. Not only that, I was then able to play tennis again, to ski without pain, and to walk endlessly. What a lesson I learned! We do not need to seek the answers to our challenges from someone outside of ourselves. Now I look for guidance and all of the solutions to so-called problems *within my Self.* Yes, this is a practical teaching!

- **Do you have your stream of income insured against a possible future disability?**

- **If you are married with few financial assets, does your husband have adequate life insurance?**

- **Are you familiar with how the purchase of long-term care insurance may be of benefit?**

- **Are you choosing a healthy lifestyle with good eating habits, exercise and meditation?**

- **Do you identify with Nature and enjoy its rejuvenating qualities?**

- **When you are ill, do you first try to determine what is causing it, or do you "hand your problem" to a medical person?**

- **Do you inform yourself by doing research when you have a health problem? (The Internet is great resource.)**

CHAPTER

Integrating Inflation Protection

"Purchasing Power of $1.00 (with 4% inflation) in 1997
dollars: 2002: 82 cents; 2007: 68 cents; 2012: 56 cents; and
2017: 46 cents."

PORTFOLIO MANAGEMENT CONSULTANTS (PMC, INC.)

Inflation-Adjusted Return

To offset the fact that our money is buying less and less of the same goods and services each year, we must include inflation in our calculations. In order to have a real financial gain, we have to obtain a return sufficient to cover inflation. The amount we net after inflation is termed the "inflation-adjusted return."

Experts are forecasting low inflation for perhaps the next 10 years, therefore I feel that 3% is probably safe to use for that period of time. After that, who knows? The average inflation rate from 1926-1998 was 3.08%. However in the 1970s inflation rose to 13%, causing investors to barely keep ahead.

Charts showing the escalating cost of items that we use in our everyday life are plentiful. The one on the next page might help you understand why it is so important to integrate inflation protection into your financial planning. Fill in the missing numbers for what the cost is today and for what you think the cost might be when you retire. From this exercise, you can see the ever decreasing purchasing power of your retirement dollars.

On the next page we also see a graph depicting the rate of returns on different asset classes with regard to inflation.

	1970	1980	TODAY	AT RETIREMENT
Postage stamp	$0.06	$0.15	_____	_____
Loaf of bread	0.23	.43	_____	_____
Automobile	3,400.00	6,900.00	_____	_____
Average home	25,600.00	64,000.00	_____	_____

From this graph we can easily see that cash and cash equivalents barely kept pace with inflation. Bonds did a little better. However, when we factor in the effect of taxes, it is possible that neither one kept pace with inflation.

HOW HAVE VARIOUS ASSET CLASSES KEPT PACE WITH INFLATION?

One of the key tests of investment success is your *real* return—
your rate of return over and above inflation.

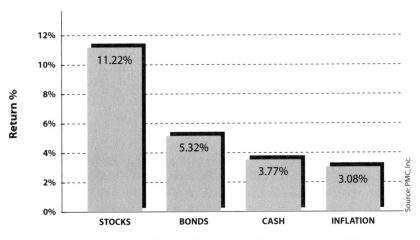

Annualized Rate of Return and Inflation 1926-1998

One method of understanding how inflation will erode your retirement nest egg is to use the Rule of 72, which is illustrated in the examples that follow and the graph on the next page.

Example 1   **Assumption: Inflation of 6%**
Divide 72 by 6. (6% is only slightly above the average inflation of 5.6% experienced from 1970 to 1995.) The answer we get is 12. That means that if we had an average of 6% a year inflation, 12 years from now, you would need $6,000 to buy the same goods and services that you can purchase today for $3,000.

Example 2   **Assumption: Inflation of 4.75%**
Divide 72 by 4.75. (4.75% is lower than the average inflation rate that we experienced from 1970 to 1995, but higher than what is currently being forecast for 1996 through 2005.) The number we get is a little more than 15. The graph below illustrates this scenario.

HOW INFLATION AFFECTS ANNUAL SPENDING REQUIREMENTS

This illustration is based on an annual inflation rate of approximately 4.75%.

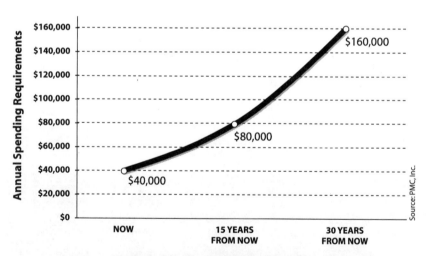

Increase in spending requirements over 30 years

We see that if today we need $40,000 annually to live, in just 15 years, it would take a little over $80,000, in 30 years around $160,000.

Although 4.75% is considered a normal inflation, I close this section with an example of a relatively low inflation assumption— 3%:

Example 3   Assumption: Inflation of 3%
Again, using the Rule of 72, divide 72 by 3. We come up with 24 years for our lifestyle to be cut in half.

Yes, I realize those 24 years sound like a long time. However my parents had a 25-year retirement, and then my mother entered an extended care facility. The costs for her care started at $40,000 a year, and when she needed additional medicine and a caregiver, the costs were closer to $100,000 a year. The message here is that it is best to have too much money than too little.

Longevity

Inflation is not the sole culprit; longevity is also a concern. People all over the world are living longer. Here in the US, a baby girl has an average life expectancy of 81, a baby boy of 74. And half of us will live well beyond those ages. Also, once we reach 65, our life expectancy increases dramatically. According to the US Census Bureau in a statistical brief published in May, 1995: "Once we reach age 65, we can expect to live 17 more years." The very fact that women live longer must mandate that they take control over their financial lives.

Not only are we living longer, our expectations regarding our standard of living have become higher. Therefore the amount of money needed for a dignified retirement has been growing steadily. Retirees are staying active well into their late 70s. They feel and appear younger than yesterday's retirees. These are the "young-old" that American psychologist B. F. Skinner wrote about many years ago. If we doubt that people act and look younger today than they did not so very long ago, we are reminded that Whistler's mother was only 58 when the artist painted his famous portrait of her.

Although the amount of money needed in retirement is increasing for everyone, the actual percentage of pre-retirement income needed in retirement depends on previous earnings as well as lifestyle. In general, you will need a higher percentage of your pre-retirement income, 70 to 80%, if you earned under $50,000, and a smaller percentage, 50 to 60%, if you earned above that amount. But keep in mind that if you rely on a "fixed" income, your lifestyle will be lowered each year because of inflation.

Adopting a lower lifestyle may be difficult. In my financial planning practice, I noticed that most individuals spend up to the amount they make. As stated earlier, some individuals spend more years in retirement than they do working. The average age of retirement is currently 59½. The reality is that if you retire then or earlier, your retirement income stream is likely to be cut in half by inflation long before you have become inactive.

Rate Shopping

Rate shopping is another reason for financial failure that we could add to those already on our list. By this we mean that individuals often pay more attention to what interest rate they are earning than to whether they are actually getting ahead financially considering inflation and taxes. The "real" return (deducting for inflation) during the period cited earlier, 1926-1998, of various assets was Cash Equivalents: 0.69%, Bonds 2.24% and Stocks 8.14%. In the next paragraph is an example concerning one of these cash equivalents, CDs.

The tendency to rate shop shows up in investors with closed minds. They invest heavily in Certificates of Deposit (CDs), still remembering that back in 1982 CDs were earning 21%. Conveniently they forget inflation was rampant. If they had factored in the inflation rate as well as taxes, which were as high as 70%, people would have realized back then that they were probably just breaking even with CDs at 21%.

"Rate shoppers" still do not factor in taxes or inflation when determining their net rate of return. Banks no longer offer toasters, etc., etc., to entice the rate shoppers, however Christopher Hayes estimates that 75% of women are still choosing to invest in bank-type investments, including CDs. Are you among them?

This investment tendency among women continues in spite of the evidence in the first chart above. It graphically shows that stocks (over the period 1926-1998—72 years, measured by the S&P Index) returned between five and almost eight times what cash equivalents did.

Here's some additional information gleaned from the chart: Bonds, based on the annualized rate of return for the Ibbotson Associates "Intermediate-Term (up to 10 years) Government Bond Index" were not as good an investment as stocks. (Ibbotson Associates is a widely recognized research firm that puts out reports on various investments.)

And although bond returns were high during the late 70s and 80s, over a 60-year period, they have returned much less than the 5.6% of recent times.

AND note that the chart does not indicate the reduction due to taxes. Remember, government bonds are taxable at the federal level, and although these investments are not taxed at the state level, this is often a worthless benefit since some areas do not have a state tax—e.g. Florida. This will be addressed in the following chapter, "Creating a Tax Favored Environment."

Growth Type Investing

Knowledge of the lower rate of return for government bonds is only part of the story. Stocks are perceived to have more volatility than bonds, thus to be more risky. From the chart below, we can see the years that have been negative since 1945.

However, as the chart points out, over a period of 54 years, there have been very few years with negative returns for stocks. The last down year for the S&P was in 1990. In reality, stocks that were held over any five-year period from 1949 to 1999 would have given a positive return. The successful investor uses both stocks and bonds and invests for the long haul.

STOCKS CAN HAVE NEGATIVE RETURNS

Since World War II, the US stock market has had some years
with significant negative returns.

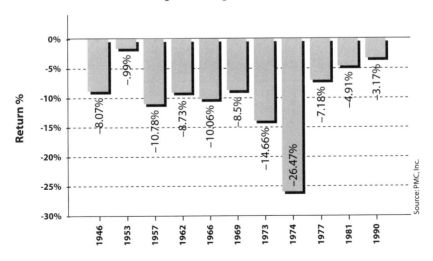

Source: PMC, Inc.

The graph below will give you a better idea of just how risky stocks have been. It shows how many quarters were positive as well as how many quarters were negative for the S&P 500 (a basket of 500 of the largest capitalized stocks in the US) from 1972 until the end of 1997.

From the graph, it is easy to see that "up" quarters far outranked the "down" quarters. The important thing is to invest for the long haul and not be concerned when the market turns down. The market is just like nature; it has ebb and flow. The message that you should be getting is that it is wisest to have a large percentage of your investment dollars in equity (stock), which signifies real growth over the long run. Hopefully you are not among the 75% of women who have their savings in bank accounts and T-bills.

And to prove our point that stocks are "a girl's best friend," we end with one more graph, which shows that even though stocks have some negative years, they usually reverse themselves over a twelve-month period. Having said this, I must add that I still do not advise a holding period of less than three years.

INVESTING IN A SINGLE ASSET CLASS IS NOT THE ANSWER

Number of Up Quarters: 76   Number of Down Quarters: 28
Maximum Up: 22.95%   Maximum Down: -25.15%

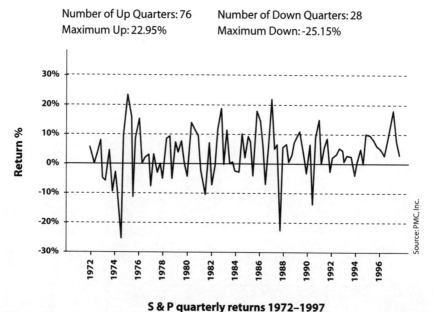

S & P quarterly returns 1972–1997

HISTORICALLY, NEGATIVE RETURNS HAVE BEEN REVERSED OVER TIME

In most cases, from 1946 to 1998, the losses of the prior year
were fully erased in the next twelve months.

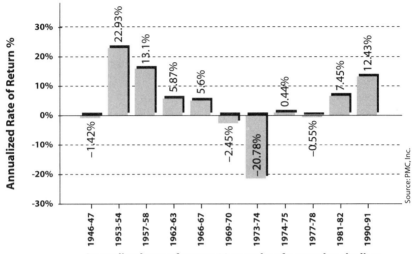

Annualized rate of return 12 months after market decline

- Were you surprised at how much the prices of everyday items had gone up?
- Are you practicing different ways to use the Rule of 72?
- Is longevity a trait in your family?
- Are you still keeping your retirement in taxable low-yielding accounts?
- Did the graph showing the up and down quarters for the S&P surprise you?
- Are your investments inflation-protected?
- Do you now see that over the long haul stocks tend to provide more inflation protection than CDs and government bonds?

Creating a Tax-Favored Environment

"If you are in the 36% federal tax bracket, and the 2.5% inflation is still holding, your after-tax inflation return on a 5% investment is .70%."

MARY F. IVINS, CFP, 1999

Another important variable to calculate into our investment return is the amount of taxes we pay. What we have left to invest after taxes is more important than what we earn. This is determined by how well we do our tax planning. In this chapter, we will address federal, state and sales taxes. We will also cover some tax-saving techniques, tax-savvy terminology and tax-wise investments.

Federal Tax Laws

We have seen erratic government policy regarding taxes. When the Reagan administration gave us a 28% tax bracket, we had to wonder, "How long will it last?" Now we know. Although you might not have realized it, we experienced one of the highest tax raises under our current president, Bill Clinton. According to my CPA, Janice Heller, the Revenue Reconciliation Act of 1993:

- Added the 36% tax bracket for years after 1992,

- Added the 10% surtax, i.e., the 39.6% bracket,

- Made permanent the itemized deduction limitation and phase-out of personal exemptions,

- Increased the maximum portion of Social Security benefits taxable to 85% for years after 1993,

- Repealed the Medicare wage base cap of $135,000 beginning in 1994, and

- Set up 2-tiered AMT (26% for first $175,000; 28% above $175,000).

You can view revisions in the tax law in different ways. If one uses the metaphor of water running under a bridge to represent taxes, you can see that one could raise the water (tax rates), which increases the amount of taxes on the same amount of income. Or you could lower the bridge by reducing or eliminating the number of ways to legally reduce taxes— limiting deductions, exemptions, credits, etc. The latest tax law revisions lowered the bridge. The government took away exemptions, raised the percentage used to calculate the Alternative Minimum Tax to 26-28%, and reduced the income level at which one is forced to use the AMT.

Yes, the government knows that increasing taxes by raising the tax bracket percentages, which it did slightly, might meet with citizen opposition. However, by hiding the increased taxes by lowering the bridge (taking away exemptions, etc.), individuals are less aware of the huge tax bite that prevents them from getting ahead.

Furthermore, more US citizens will be forced to use the more costly AMT method of calculating their taxes. The Alternative Minimum Tax is calculated differently. Many items that otherwise would have been tax-deductible or untaxed, like tax-exempt income under the regular way of figuring your tax are added back to determine the amount of taxable income.

As the tax law now stands, the middle class will be using the costlier method of the Alternative Minimum Tax (AMT) in a few years. The reason is that the income level that forces one to use AMT is not indexed. In other words, as the individual's income escalates based on pay raises, the set income level (not indexed for inflation) will be surpassed:

Example   An individual who would be in the 28% tax bracket for regular taxes might pay $5,000 in taxes. However, if her/his income, figured to include adding back what are known as "tax preference" items (see Glossary), qualifies her/him for the AMT, she/he will pay 26%-28% on that income. Although this might seem that this could be lower than the regular tax rate, it would be higher because of the lack of exemptions, etc.

In addition, although the amount of our income taxed for general Social Security (FICA) taxes is still limited, the Medicare tax of 1.45% is levied on an individual's total income—no longer is there a limit. An individual making $100,000 used to see an empty space after "FICA" on his pay stub after his income was above a certain amount (indexed for inflation). Now that space is never empty. She/he continues paying 1.45% on any income over the Social Security wage base.

Currently Social Security taxes are the fastest growing tax levied in the US. The total tax stands at 15.3%. The employer withholds 6.2%, and an additional 1.45% for Medicare, and has to match the percentage withheld from the employee. Take a look at your W-2 to see how much you are paying in FICA each year. The self-employed individual pays 15.3% on their net—after business expenses—1099 income. This includes a 12.4% component for old-age, survivors and disability insurance (OSADI) and the 2.9% component for hospital insurance (Medicare).

State and Sales Taxes

It is not only federal taxes that zap our ability to get ahead. It is important to look at all of the taxes that we are paying in order to understand the impact on our investment results. All taxes reduce our actual return. People in the lower income brackets pay more as a percentage of income in state and sales taxes. I explain why below.

Often the state levies high utility taxes. One would expect households to use roughly about the same amount of utilities. But the taxes represent more when stated as a percentage of income for the poor. And the dollar amount may actually be more as well, because often the poor live in inadequately insulated homes. Sales taxes are similarly unfair as most of the income of poor people is used for purchasing necessities. Therefore they pay a larger percentage of their income in sales tax. In Illinois, unlike New Jersey and some other states, food purchases also have a sales tax.

In the chart below, representing the average amount individuals pay for the various types of taxes, I have used the sales tax for downtown Chicago. Your sales tax may be somewhat less, however your state tax might be higher. You'll notice that the FICA or Social Security tax percentage is huge. Remember that although your portion may not seem bad at 6.2% + 1.45%, your employer must pay 7.65% for the total of 15.3%.

A REALISTIC LOOK AT THE TAX PERCENTAGES				
Types of taxes	Federal	State	FICA	Sales
Percentage	15-39.6%	3-7%	7.65-15.3%	8.75%

To begin to understand how difficult it is to make real gains in our assets, examine the two examples given below:

Example 1   With a 4% inflation and a 40% total tax, we must earn 12.5% on our investments to net a 2% real gain.

Example 2   With a 2.5% inflation (approximate current rate) and 36% Federal tax bracket, our after-tax/inflation return on a 5% investment is .70%.

Tax Advice

Unfortunately it is commonly up to us to determine if we are paying too much in taxes. Quite often accountants are "reactive" and not "proactive." They assist us with filing our income taxes—often using computers—but seldom pay attention to offering us advice on ways to lower our taxes. I have been fortunate. Janice Heller, CPA, was attracted into my life when I first started my business career. Although one year I calculated my own taxes in order to better understand all of the schedules, etc., I still had Janice look it over for errors. Undoubtedly her wealth of knowledge has saved me many dollars in taxes. Thank you, Universe, for putting Janice Heller on my path.

Stockbrokers also do little in this area. They are usually more interested in making a sale than concerning themselves with their clients' tax situations. A story to illustrate this is from my second marriage. The man I married had a stockbroker. The broker called and told us how great a certain preferred stock was. This is a stock that a company issues with a fixed rate of interest—more like a bond. And similar to a bond, the underlying value does not fluctuate much. This type of investment is mostly for those who are psychologically adverse to the ups and downs of common stock.

Although perceived as less risky than common stock, the truth is that there is still a risk involved in an investment in a preferred stock, even though its price fluctuates less than the price for common stock. If the company would go into bankruptcy, the holders of the preferred stock would receive their money back only after the holders of the company's bonds. If there was enough money, the common stockholders would be the last to receive compensation on their investment.

When I noticed that the preferred stock's value didn't change much, I called the broker to ask why. He responded, "Well, it is a safe investment, and it's paying 8%." I then asked, "Did you ask if we were looking for income and a 'safe' investment?" The broker started to bristle. I went on to ask, "Do you know what tax bracket we're in?" He exploded! He must have been thinking, "How dare a woman ask such intelligent questions!"

When the broker put us into this investment, he never even bothered to ask if we were risk-adverse or what tax bracket we were in. At that time there was a 50% tax bracket, and my husband was in it. Therefore the preferred stock, which had little potential for appreciation, was netting us little more than we could have received in a safer investment. Clearly a preferred stock was not an appropriate investment for us.

Tax-Saving Techniques

For all the above reasons, it is up to us to become acquainted with the legal ways to save on our taxes. As stated in Chapter 8, "Examining the Reasons Why People Fail Financially," not understanding the tax laws is another reason for financial failure. When we save tax dollars, we are creating more investment dollars. If the investments that we purchase with our tax savings are also tax-exempt or tax-deferred, we are creating even more dollars to invest and our investments therefore can grow more rapidly. A few of these tax-saving techniques/strategies are shown in the following table.

TAX-SAVING TECHNIQUES/STRATEGIES	
Avoiding:	Non-deductible, high-interest consumer loans (credit card debt)
Using:	Tax-deductible Home Equity Line of Credit (HELC) for purchases of large-ticket items
Including:	Purchases (using non-taxed dollars) of tax-deferred investments (IRAs, 401(k)s, 403(b)s, etc.)
Using:	After-tax dollars to purchase non-taxed, tax-deferred, tax-favored and tax-credited investments
Employing:	Section 1031 of the Tax Code

Avoiding: Non-deductible, high-interest consumer loans (credit card debt)

Because credit card usage is so prevalent in our society, I have addressed it often in my book. It is not difficult to understand why it would be wise to pay off any credit card debt when we receive the monthly bill. Not only is credit card debt non-deductible, it is expensive. Although many banks have reduced their credit card fees from the steep rates of over 21%, many of the retail stores still charge this amount.

But even if we round off the $.21 to $.20, we see that we are actually paying off our debt in dollars worth $1.36. In a 30% tax bracket, we have to earn $1.30 to net out the dollar. Adding the tax on $.20 ($.06) to the cost, we see where the $1.36 comes from. This is a losing situation. The best action is to always pay off your credit cards each month as they come due. If you have allowed yourself to be caught up in the credit-card frenzy, here are some techniques to use:

- Stop using credit cards immediately,

- Establish a method to pay off the debt that you already have accumulated,

- Transfer the debt from high-interest credit cards to lower-interest ones, and/or

- Consolidate your debt by re-mortgaging your home for an amount that includes your high-interest credit card debt.

If you do re-mortgage your home, never build up credit card debt again. This is a one-time fix and is not to be repeated.

Using: Tax-Deductible Home Equity Line of Credit (HELC) for purchases of large-ticket items

As has already been pointed out earlier, using credit wisely is beneficial. Since this is such an important subject, it bears repeating. When you are considering buying any large-ticket item—a new deck, room expansion, carpeting, new kitchen, appliances, new automobile, etc.—use a loan against your home equity. Recall that the name of this loan is a HELC. Also, recall that you pay interest—which is certainly lower than credit card interest and is usually tax deductible—only on the money that you actually borrow. But, again, you must discipline yourself to pay these amounts back in a timely manner.

In fact, in the case of home improvements, like room additions, it might be wiser to re-mortgage your home. Crunch the numbers. Also examine how you "feel" about taking on more long-term debt. Perhaps your current cash flow would allow you to pay off the HELC. In addition to saving taxes, the investments that you already have in place will be compounding, which has already been discussed. By using the "miracle of compounding," you will tap into the only way of accumulating money for long-term money needs. If you insist on paying cash for everything, you won't be able to take advantage of this.

Too often we are afraid of debt. As stated earlier, I usually advise my clients to take out a 30-year mortgage rather than a 15-year mortgage. I then suggest that the difference in the amount of payment between the 15-year and the 30-year mortgage be invested in a tax-exempt bond fund, which will be fully explained below under "Tax Saving Investments" and in Chapter 15, "Structuring Mutual Fund/Stock and Bond Portfolios."

The money in the tax-exempt bond fund can be used to take advantage of investment opportunities. These opportunities present themselves when the market goes down. Unfortunately investors usually sell at these opportune times. They get nervous when their mutual fund or stock holdings begin to lose value. Even if you consider the tax-exempt bonds as an investment, you can't go wrong. Historically, these bonds have returned over 10%, considering interest and appreciation.

And if you are in a high tax bracket, this 10% is actually higher than if the 10% was taxable. The reason the return is higher than 10% for high-bracket taxpayers is that the portion that is interest comes tax-free. For example, if you are in a 30% federal tax bracket, your return is 13% (30% of 10% = 3% plus the 10%), and even the capital gains— the appreciation or growth of these funds—is taxed at a rate of 20%, which is usually lower than the individual's tax bracket. This return is usually more than the mortgage interest and certainly more than the net after-tax mortgage interest. Savvy investors know that being mortgage-free may not be in their best interests.

Including: Purchases with non-taxed dollars of tax-deferred investments (IRAs, 401(k)s, 403(b)s, etc.)

In order for you to be able to buy investments with dollars that have never been taxed, you have to invest in qualified plans. The obvious advantage of putting money into IRAs or employee savings plans is that the investment dollars have not been taxed. This means that they are discounted dollars. (In a 30% tax bracket, they would only be worth $.70.) And you don't pay current taxes on the interest (fixed accounts) or the growth plus interest and dividends (variable accounts —stocks, bonds or real estate). Taxes are deferred until distributions are taken. This tax deferment can be very beneficial even if your tax bracket is not much lower after retirement. In addition, knowing that you have a "nest egg" is psychologically healthy.

Even if you have limited financial assets and have an intermediate goal (five years) of owning your own home, you are still better off saving these dollars in a qualified plan rather than in an account purchased with after-tax dollars. The taxes that are deferred add up in five years. If you use a Roth IRA, which is bought with after-tax dollars, you still have the advantage of tax deferment. And you will not be taxed on the dollars you take out as long as you leave the money in the account for five years. Another way of using money from a qualified plan for a purchase of a home is to take a loan out on your 401(k) account. Since you own the account, you are actually paying the interest back to yourself.

While on the subject of 401(k) plans, are you maximizing your contributions, i.e. putting in the maximum amount allowable under law? If that is not possible, are you at least contributing up to the company match? For instance, your company matches up to 6%. If you are only contributing 4%, you are losing big. And the other 2% your company could contribute would cost you less than 2%. The reason is that your additional 2% contribution would have been taxed if you did not put it into the plan. Therefore you have not really paid the full 2% and have still gained a substantial asset that will continue growing tax-deferred. Here's an example to help you understand this.

> **Example** By contributing the extra 2%, you are reducing your taxes. Let's say that you are in a 30% tax bracket and the dollar amount of your 2% contribution is $50. Since you get to take the $50 off of your reported income, the amount you are contributing is actually less than $50 or $35 ($50 – $15, the amount of taxes on $50.).

Thus you have $100 credited to your account ($50 = your employer's contribution and $50 = your contribution at a cost of $35 (divide the $35 by $100 to arrive at the percentage of your return—35%). And this percentage is before the $100 is invested. Let's say you earn 10% on the investment. Add that to the 35% already made on the investment and you see that you have earned 45% on your money—and the 35% is guaranteed.

To reap all of the benefits of tax-free, tax-deferred investing, don't take the money out of your IRA or company savings plans until after age 59½ or you will have to pay taxes on the full amount, plus a 10% penalty. Also, if you are in a low tax bracket, the benefit of maximizing your contribution to an IRA or company savings plan may not be there. However, in general, after you have established an emergency fund as explained in Chapter 8, it is always best to deduct an IRA contribution and to maximize your qualified plans.

> **Example** Even if you only make $15,000 a year, you wind up paying federal taxes of approximately $1,500. By reducing this amount by an IRA contribution, your taxes would be reduced by $300-400. These savings can be invested too. If you save approximately $166.67 a month in a stock growth mutual fund, at the end of 12 months, you will have your $2,000. Even if you can only save $100 a month towards

your IRA contribution that is wiser than not contributing anything.

Using: After-tax dollars to purchase non-taxed, tax-deferred, tax-favored and tax-credit investments

Non-taxed or tax-exempt bonds

Non-taxed or tax-exempt investments come in many forms. Here, we will only examine the individual bond. In a later chapter, we will fully explain non-individual tax-exempt bonds. A municipality to finance an improvement issues individual bonds. The return on this bond investment would be free of Federal taxes, and it can be free of state taxes as well if purchased in the state where you reside. This latter purchase would result in what is termed as "double tax-free." Below is an example:

Example Assumptions: 31% federal tax, 5% state tax, 6% return on 20-year AAA municipal bond (Note: This yield is not currently available.)
Bond issued and purchased outside of state where investor resides would return taxable equivalent of 8.70%. Bond issued and purchased in state where investor resides would return taxable equivalent of 9.15%

Deferred annuities (tax-deferred)

Unlike the interest on CDs and the dividends and capital gains on mutual funds, which must be declared on your 1040 each year, the appreciation of your deferred annuity portfolio grows tax-deferred and is not taxed until the time of withdrawal. Although prior to August of 1982, distributions up to your cost basis (initial investment) were considered a return of capital (and were non-taxable), now any withdrawals above your cost basis are immediately taxed.

And although distributions from a deferred annuity taken before age 59½ are penalized by 10%, this investment is still quite attractive. The money grows tax-deferred and the fixed rate in "fixed-rate" annuities is usually 2-3% higher than CD rates. The variable rate in "variable" annuities is tied to the results of the stock and bond market. Historically variable annuities have done quite well. Like a CD, there is no charge to get involved, however there usually are penalties if you terminate the contract before maturity (CDs) or before the penalty-free period (deferred annuities).

The benefit of the tax deferral of the appreciation within the annuity really becomes dramatic over a long period. Here is an example how the tax deferment can fit into your long-term investment strategy:

DIFFERENCE BETWEEN RETURN ON TAX-DEFERRED ANNUITY AND TAXABLE INVESTMENT GROWING AT 8%			
INVESTMENT	FEDERAL & STATE TAX RATE	TIME HELD	ROI
$10,000 Tax-Deferred Annuity	33%	20 years 30 years	$46,610 $100,627
$10,000 Taxable Investment	33%	20 years 30 years	$27,562 $45,759

Immediate Annuities (tax-favored; see under "Tax-Savvy Terminology," p. 151)

Tax Credit Investments (tax reduction; see under Tax-Savvy Terminology, p. 151, and under "Tax-Wise Investments," pp. 152-153)

Employing Section 1031 of the Internal Revenue Tax Code
Another tax-saving technique (named after a section of the IRS code) is known as a "1031 exchange." If you have purchased real estate that has appreciated as an investment, you can defer indefinitely the capital gains taxes if you exchange—a 1031 exchange—the appreciated property for one of a higher value. To do this, not only must the new investment property be worth more than the one that you are exchanging, but you must use every dollar that you receive from the sale of the first property for the purchase of the new one.

For instance, I once knew of a couple who had purchased a home in Colorado. At the time that the husband was changing jobs and the couple was moving to New Jersey, the real estate values in Colorado were depressed. This couple did not want to sell the Colorado property; it was worth less than they had paid for it. Instead they rented their former home, thus it became an investment. Years later, when the property values returned to their former prices, the couple exchanged the Colorado property for an investment property on the New Jersey shore.

This accomplished three things: (1) The couple had both a tax deduction and limited use of this shore home for vacations while the husband still worked; (2) They would never have to pay the capital gains tax due from the sale of the first property once it became their permanent home at retirement; and, (3) Their heirs would not pay any capital gains tax if they sold the property before any additional appreciation.

All inherited property, including investments and real estate, etc., takes a "stepped-up" value, valued at day of death or six months later. Therefore, there are no taxes due. However, property given in life takes on the donor's cost basis and when the asset is sold, capital gains taxes are due. If the above reinvestment technique would benefit your financial plan, contact your CPA or a real estate/tax lawyer.

Tax-Savvy Terminology

Some of the terms used above may be foreign to you. Let's look at them individually:

Non-deductible interest

If we itemized deductions years ago, credit card interest was tax-deductible. Now it is non-deductible.

Tax-deductible items

If you use the long form for calculating your taxes, there are certain items that are tax-deductible. These items include mortgage interest, real estate taxes, and state and sales tax, which go on Schedule A—Itemized Deductions. The amount of your business expenses that exceeds your business income from Schedule C—Profit or Loss from Business, is tax-deductible. Then, on Schedule E—Supplemental Income and Loss, the rental losses on properties you own, plus other business expenses—not reimbursed—that you incurred as an employee for things like auto, travel expenses, and 50% of your meals, etc., are tax-deductible. Just remember, although you do save some taxes on the above-mentioned items, all but depreciation on property (Schedule E), cost money. In order to get the tax deduction, you first have to spend the dollars. The amount you save is the taxes you would have paid on the listed amounts.

Non-taxed dollars

We purchase traditional IRAs, 401(k)s, 403(b)s, etc., with dollars that have never been taxed—non-taxed dollars. Therefore we consider these to be "discounted" or "partial" dollars.

Tax-deferred

Investments bought in the qualified plans above grow "tax-deferred" until we take distributions. Then they are fully taxed. As explained above, the appreciation in a deferred annuity also grows tax-deferred. However this does not include the appreciation in mutual fund assets if the fund manager takes distributions. Even if we don't physically take possession of these distributions, we still must pay regular income taxes on the interest and/or dividends and capital gains taxes on other distributions in the tax year distributions were taken.

As mentioned, all disbursements from deferred annuities up until our cost basis are taxed until our cost basis (the original amount of our investment) is reached. And should we die and leave an annuity to an heir, they would pay regular income tax on the amount received. It is important for us to be aware of what money is taxable at the capital gains rate, currently topped at 20%, and what is taxed at our regular income-tax rate. Usually it is better to pay capital gains taxes than regular income taxes.

After-tax dollars

These dollars have already been taxed. As pointed out earlier, they are expensive dollars. Depending on the investment, they are not taxed again when we take disbursements. Exceptions to this are deferred annuities bought after 1982 and dividends and interest we receive from corporations. The dollars paid out in dividends and interest from the corporation's profits have already been taxed; however under present law, the individual who receives them must pay another tax. The exceptions are examples of "double-taxed" dollars.

Tax-exempt

When we purchase tax-exempt bonds, we do not pay taxes on the interest received—whether it's left in the account or taken. It is "tax-exempt." However, if the fund manager cashes in some of the bonds and takes a capital gain (from appreciation), we have to pay capital gains taxes on this 1099 income. When we take partial distributions from an account, again we do not pay taxes on the tax-free interest paid out or accumulated. However, if the fund has appreciated, we will pay capital gains taxes on a portion of what we receive.

Tax-favored

We have already discussed "deferred annuities," in which we leave the funds to grow and we continue to own the contract. Now we take a look at "immediate annuities," from which we start to take income and where we have sold the contract back to the insurance company. When we purchase immediate annuities with after-tax dollars, the payment we receive is "tax-favored." This means that up to 85% of the distributions are not taxed. On a qualified immediate annuity—like our pension plans—we pay income tax on every dollar we receive because the corporation who funded our pension has never paid taxes on these dollars. It deducts all pension contributions from its profits.

Tax credits

On line 47 of your 1040, you will notice a space to list credits. This is where you would put the number calculated by the tax-credit firm you are invested with. Notice that this is below line 40 where you have listed your "tax." What this means is that a tax credit is not a tax write-off where you get a percentage of a dollar back; this is a dollar-for-dollar reduction in your taxes.

Real and marginal tax rates

The "real" rate of taxation is found by dividing the amount you paid in taxes by the amount of your income. Your marginal tax rate is how an additional dollar of income would be taxed. You can't do much about your W-2 income, however you may be able to do something about pushing yourself into the next marginal tax bracket by monitoring your bonus or moon-lighting income, etc.

In addition, when you look at a Tax Rate Schedule provided by the IRS, you will see that incomes are bracketed. Often it is to your advantage to lower your income, say by contributing to a deductible IRA, in order to lower your income bracket. Also, you might take a business expense deduction for something purchased in the current tax year but not actually paid for until the following year.

Before leaving this section, I would like to add that just because your employer deducted sufficient taxes out of your salary and you don't have to pay any additional taxes at tax time doesn't mean that you "pay no taxes." And if you do get some money back—in excess of $500 —change your W-4. Why give the government an interest-free loan? Use the money for an investment.

Tax-Wise Investments

Some of the tax-wise investments—contributions to IRAs and qualified plans, tax-free bonds, growth stock accounts and annuities—have already been discussed. However one remains: Tax Credit Programs. In 1985, the government wanted to stimulate individual savings as well as promote housing for the lower economic strata. It sponsored Tax Credit Programs. The low-income housing industry has been around for some time—about 20 years. It has been in private hands, i.e. not in government programs. Since its inception, the industry has been very profitable. That is the reason that when these programs were established the government decided to place its confidence in the private sector.

Originally these credits averaged 15% of the investor's investment. Currently the percentage is somewhat lower. In other words, if an individual invested $10,000 into these government-sponsored, low-income-housing tax credit programs, she/he would receive over a period of 10 years the equivalent of a 15% return each year ($1,500), or a total of $15,000. The yearly amount would vary, but would average $1,500. The amount varies because not all properties come on stream at the same time; there is a "ramping up" of the interest rates. However, after the investor's dollars have been invested for three full years, the full interest rate should be attained. Each year, the investor will either reduce her/his tax liability by the amount of the tax credit or if fully funded for her/his tax liability, would ask for a tax refund.

Before 1994, Congress had to approve these Tax Credit programs each year. Since 1994, when Congress made funding for the tax-credit programs permanent, more and more developers have been getting involved. Two things result from this additional involvement: (1) The prices for the properties have escalated, and it is no longer possible to get a 15% annual return—more like 10-11%; and (2) There is a ready market for these complexes when they have received all of their tax credits. It now is possible for the same syndicate to refinance and start all over again with the same properties even if the qualifying period of 15 years is not finished.

This permanence of the tax credits adds to the safety of these investments. In addition, the units are built in outlying areas—not in central cities. The graying of America will cause the need for this type of housing to swell. And since approximately half of these townhouses are specifically built for the elderly—one of the best kinds of tenants—and about one-third of the other half are occupied by the elderly, there is little downside risk. In addition to the need being present, the tax credits are budgeted for and pre-funded for 10 years. Although the IRS issues the credits, the Treasury administers the program. Therefore the credits cannot be taken back. To do so would be like issuing Treasury notes and then not honoring their coupons.

The key here is to go with a company that has a track record of success in this industry. Also, check out what percentage of the funding is coming from government mortgages. These usually have more astringent regulations than conventional private mortgages. In addition, make certain that the properties are geographically diversified. Recently we have witnessed waves of recession, i.e. when the East and West Coasts were booming, the Rust Belt was hurting. Then the Midwest started to recover while the economies of the two coasts went downwards. Since no one can foretell what the future economic situation will be like or when the opportune time will be to sell these properties, it is best to have some in many geographic areas.

Even though in Chapter 14, you will find this type of investment to be almost at the top of the risk/reward pyramid, I highly recommend it. The reason that it is near the top with regard to risk is that the SEC has labeled it a "limited partnership." However, unlike investments in limited partnerships, these are structured entirely differently and the return is a promise issued by the Treasury— not a private organization.

In concluding this section on tax-wise investments, let me add that I usually advise that individuals buy a tax-free mutual bond fund, which will be fully explained in Chapter 15, "Structuring Mutual Fund/ Stock and Bond Portfolios," as a backup to their emergency fund. By combining taxable, cash-equivalent investments with a tax-free bond account, you will have immediate access to cash for an emergency, and you can access the tax-free account if you need more emergency money.

Also, if you think that a variable deferred annuity would fit into your investment strategy, plan to contribute on a monthly basis in order to take advantage of dollar-cost-averaging (explained later), but choose an annuity that does not start the penalty clock each time you make a deposit.

Again, it is very important to maximize the return on your investments by employing as many tax-saving techniques as are legal and practical. The knowledge contained in this section is a "must" to master.

- **Do you know how much you are paying in federal Income Tax?**

- **Do you know what your marginal and your real tax rate is?**

- **Are you using every method to reduce your state and sales taxes? (Hint: Goods sent across state borders usually don't have state taxes if there is no similar facility in your jurisdiction.)**

- **Are you relying too much on your accountant/broker to save you money on taxes?**

- **Are you employing some or all of the tax-saving techniques?**

- **Have you familiarized yourself with the tax-savvy terminology?**

- **Are you including tax-wise investments as part of your financial planning strategies?**

Understanding Return on Investment (ROI)

"You can only get poor quickly; getting rich takes time."

GRACE W. WEINSTEIN,
Money Matters: A Woman's Guide to Financial Well-being, 1998

The final variable in the Success Formula is Return on Investment (ROI). In this chapter, I will show you how to dramatically maximize your return on your investments by incorporating some important investment conventions. These include dollar-cost averaging, diversification, asset allocation and leveraging. Don't worry if any of these concepts are new to you. Each of these principles will be fully explained in the current chapter. By combining these conventions with different methods of investing, you can achieve remarkable financial success.

In Chapter 15, "Structuring Mutual Fund/Stock and Bond Portfolios" you will be given pointers on how to choose the right mutual fund as well as suitable stocks and bonds. The lessons that you have learned thus far will help you to do this.

Dollar-Cost Averaging

This technique for improving your investment results is based on a mathematical axiom. Simply stated, it says that through periodic staged investments, you will gain the benefit of buying more shares of stock or of mutual funds when the price is low and fewer shares when the price is high.

The table that we will use to illustrate this concept is for shares in a mutual fund. However, shares of a company's stock can also be bought with dollar-cost averaging through what is known as a dividend re-investment plan or DRP, which we already referred to. The way that the DRP works is that the investor signs an agreement with the company to have her/his dividends reinvested in the company's stock. In addition, the investor can send in extra money for the purchase of the company's stock. This is a great way to accumulate stock in a company you believe in as well as to always pay less than the average cost per share.

Compare the dollar-cost-averaging method where money is invested periodically with that of making a one-time investment. Here is a table to help you understand this valuable concept:

	ONE-TIME INVESTMENT COMPARED TO DOLLAR-COST AVERAGING OVER A PERIOD OF 10 MONTHS					
	One-time investment			**Dollar-cost averaging**		
MONTH	**AMOUNT PAID**	**COST PER SHARE**	**NO. SHARES PURCHASED**	**AMOUNT PAID**	**COST PER SHARE**	**NO. SHARES PURCHASED**
1	$1,500	$6	250	$150	$6	25
2	0			150	8	18.75
3	0			150	10	15
4	0			150	10	15
5	0			150	8	18.75
6	0			150	6	25
7	0			150	4	37.5
8	0			150	2	75
9	0			150	2	75
10	0			150	4	37.5
TOTALS	**$1,500**	**Avg. $6.00**	**250**	**$1,500**	**Avg. $4.38**	**342.5**

With dollar-cost averaging, the average cost per share = $4.38 and the number of shares purchased is 342.50. Without dollar-cost averaging, the cost per share is $6.00 and the number of shares purchased is 250.

The table traces your purchases. It might be difficult to believe that you actually benefit when the share price goes lower. Too often when the investor sees that the share price is going lower, she/he sells the shares. The commitment of a certain dollar amount each month will help you avoid the impulse to push the panic button and sell.

Diversification

Dollar-cost averaging can easily be applied to the purchasing of mutual funds, and with this type of investment, there is an added benefit—*diversification*. Since a mutual fund is a bundle of different stocks, bonds and cash equivalents, diversification is always present.

None of the conventions discussed in this chapter is more important than this one. It has been statistically proven that more than 91% of the success in investing comes not from picking "winners" all of the time, but rather from having a diverse portfolio. Let's examine two portfolios.

HOW ASSET CLASS DIVERSIFICATION WORKS

Performance of two portfolios over the 20 years ending in 1997.

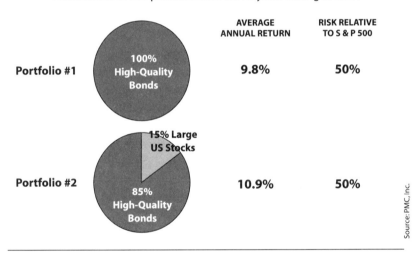

Portfolio 1 Assumptions: 100% invested in high-quality bonds (Bonds that are rated better than BBB by Standard & Poor's—see Glossary). Period covered is 20 years, ending in 1997.
Annual average return is 9.8%.

Portfolio 2 Assumptions: 85% invested in high-quality bonds. 15% invested in large US Stocks. Period covered is 20 years, ending in 1997.
Annual average return is 10.9%.

The pie charts above illustrate how very important it is to hold more than one asset class. Although we will be addressing the issue of risk in the next chapter, you should note what this graph has to say. By including only 15% of the portfolio in stocks, the risk was not increased. Yet the return shows a significant boost, from 9.8% to 10.9%.

An even better method of injecting the safety factor of diversification into your portfolio is by including some international stocks. This is so because quite often the corollary between the return on international and domestic stocks is low. What this means is that when our domestic (US) stocks are going up, the international stocks tend to be going down and vice versa.

The international markets are expanding. We are truly in a global economy. In 1986, the US market represented almost two-thirds of the world's capitalization (the total value of all good and services produced in the entire world). Today it represents about one-third of the world's capitalization.

From the graph below, you can see that the highest return occurred when all asset classes were held—including international stocks. Therefore I would recommend that at least 20% of your mutual fund/stock portfolio be in international stocks. While you can include

THE BENEFITS OF GLOBAL DIVERSIFICATION, 1972-1997

Increase the Number of Asset Classes—Improve Results

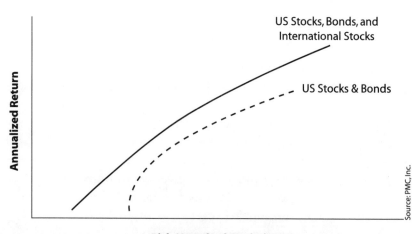

Source: PMC, Inc.

your holdings in multinational US corporations—those that derive a large part of their income from the overseas markets—it is still important to hold stocks of foreign lands.

This can be done easily through mutual funds specializing in international stocks like Franklin/Templeton. Foreign stocks can also be purchased in a closed-end international fund or through ADRs (American Depository Receipts). ADRs are stock certificates of foreign companies sold on the American stock exchanges. Since the individual does not have personal dealings with the foreign exchanges, this makes it easier for US citizens to purchase foreign stocks.

In a closed-end fund, the manager buys stocks, usually of one country, bundles them into a fund, and then sells shares of the portfolio. The shares can be selling at either a "premium" to their net asset value or at a "discount." Not too many years ago, the shares in the Korean Fund were selling at a "premium," i.e. higher than the NAV. (The NAV is calculated by dividing the total price for all of the stocks by the number of shares in the fund.) Today because of all of the economic trouble in the Pacific Basin it is selling at a "discount." If you believe in the adage, "Buy on bad news," this is a good time to purchase these shares. I predict that the Pacific Rim countries' economies will again flourish.

Asset Allocation

Asset allocation is a first cousin to diversification, however it is not the same thing. Asset allocation is the creation of a diversified portfolio by combining different types of investments. This is in contrast to diversifying your portfolio by buying different investments within the same asset class i.e., various types of stocks, bonds or mutual funds.

With asset allocation, your portfolio will contain different types of assets—stocks, bonds, real estate, non-US stocks and cash and cash equivalents. In addition, you would have a certain percentage of your portfolio in each of these asset classes. Although most of your return in an investment portfolio will be determined by diversification within each asset class, you must first create a portfolio that contains all the asset classes—or as many as you can afford.

Often investors, women in particular, are fearful of the gyrations in the value of their investment portfolios. Since the various asset classes usually act differently in any given market, combining them will tend to keep the value of your portfolio more constant. The perceived risk is reduced. Also, it is important to always look at the average return. You can get this figure by adding up the total dollar return on all of your invested assets and dividing the resulting figure by the prior year's total dollar value. Here's an example to assist your understanding:

Example   **Assumptions: Prior year's value of portfolio is $20,000. Portfolio holdings: 65% in US stocks (25% return), 20% in non-US stocks (-8% return), 10% in bonds (5% return) and 5% in cash equivalents (3% return). See graphic representation of the portfolio below.**

To figure the return on your investment, do the following calculations:

65% of $20,000 ($13,000) is US stocks. A 25% return =	$3,250
10% of $20,000 ($2,000) is bonds. A 5% return =	$100
5% of $20,000 ($1,000) is cash equivalents. A 3% return =	$30
Total positive return =	**$3,380**
20% of $20,000 ($4,000) is Non-US stocks. A –8% return =	–$320
Total net return	**$3,060**
Divide this by the total dollar amount of last year's portfolio ($20,000) to calculate return on investment =	÷$20,000 **15.3%**

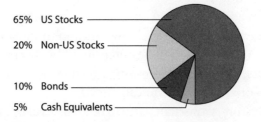

HYPOTHETICAL INVESTMENT PORTFOLIO

65% US Stocks

20% Non-US Stocks

10% Bonds

5% Cash Equivalents

Source: PMC, Inc.

From this example, you can see that even if one of the asset classes that you have in your portfolio performs poorly, you can still have a very nice return. And it is important to do this for each year in a 5-, 10- or 20-year time frame. One year is not enough to measure.

The type of asset allocation that you decide upon depends on your ability to accept the volatility that comes from being involved with the equity (stock) market and, somewhat, on your need for immediate income. Risk will be examined further in Chapter 14, "Grasping the Risk/Reward Pyramid." Often risk is "perceived" risk and not "real" risk. Remember that the investor does not have a "real" loss until she/he sells his investment. Until then, it is simply a "paper loss" which is nothing to be concerned about.

As you have probably already noticed, I am biased to an asset allocation that is heavily weighted to equities (stocks). The asset allocation used in the "Hypothetical Investment Portfolio" is what I recommend to my clients. As pointed out earlier, equities have had the highest return for any asset class in the last 40 years. Even when there has been high inflation, the value of the underlying businesses has increased. Using US Treasury notes or bonds as a sole investment class would not have brought anywhere near the results that would have occurred with allocating some of your assets to the stock market.

While living in New Jersey, I was fortunate to present financial seminars to the faculty at the New Jersey School of Medicine and Dentistry (UMDNJ) in Newark. In order to prepare, I had to become familiar with the state retirement plan called the TIAA/CREF. This is a program to provide academics with a good retirement income and was introduced in 1956 by Andrew Carnegie. The fixed-income or guaranteed income portion is known as the Teachers Insurance Annuity Association or TIAA. The mutual fund side is known as the College Retirement Equities Fund or CREF.

Although the equity accounts are managed by outside managers, the guaranteed portion is backed by and managed by the insurance company (TIAA). You may be familiar with a guaranteed account in your 401(k) plan. The sponsoring firm guarantees you a certain percentage of return. Depending on the interest rates currently available, it sets rates of return generally on an annual basis. Since often these rates are a "rolling average"—ones taken from about five years of rates

—the person who chooses a guaranteed account usually receives a rate that is higher than the current interest rate.

A study of the investment results of the TIAA/CREF accounts was done after they were in existence for 40 years. If the academic had placed $1.00 in the guaranteed fixed account, he would have had $88 for his $1.00. If he had placed $1.00 in the stock account, he would have had almost 14 times more or around $1,200 for his $1.00 investment. Here is a story that supports the study's findings:

One of the attendees at my seminar was a young woman librarian. Fifteen years earlier when she joined the TIAA/CREF plan, she was so unsure of herself that she put 75% of the state's contribution of 6% of her salary into the guaranteed fixed account and 25% of it into the stock account. At the time of our meeting, she said that the amount in each account was about equal. In other words, even though each pay period she had invested 50% more into the fixed account over a 15-year period, her stock account had grown to around the same amount.

I am certain that other individuals at the seminar would have benefited from her story, however she shared this with me privately. Hopefully this young lady was watching *Wall Street Week* a few years back. During the show, Louis Rukeyser asked his 99-year-old guest investment expert if he adhered to the long-lived idea that one should rebalance a portfolio (changing the percentage in each asset class) each year after reaching age 65.

According to this concept, prior to age 65, the recommended allocation was 65% in stocks and 35% in bonds. (Technically cash and cash equivalents are not investments). After retirement, for each year over 65, the person would subtract a percentage point from the stock allocation and add it to the bond allocation. The 99-year-old active investment counselor replied, "No, I have 100% of my assets in the stock market."

Leveraging

In actuality, investing in growth assets, usually perceived as more risky and seldom furnishing current income, is prudent. This is a form of leveraging. You are making a small amount of money do the work of a larger amount. As stated earlier, with the initial divorce settlement from my first divorce—$10,000, I bought my first real estate investment. The year was 1979. The property, a condo with a separate garage in Downers Grove, Illinois, cost $43,000, and I used the $10,000 as a down payment.

Today the condo is worth approximately $80,000. Using a financial calculator—and not deducting for capital gains—the return on my original $10,000 would be in the area of 11% annually. (To arrive at this figure, enter $80,000 as a future value (FV), $10,000 as a present value (PV) and 20 as the number (n) and punch the interest "i" key.) That's a good return, however it does not tell the total story. In order to arrive at a truer picture, I would have to add the dollar amounts of the tax write-offs (deductions) that I received for the cost of the maintenance, repairs, real estate taxes, mortgage interest and depreciation during the 20 years. Considering these factors, my return on my $10,000 investment would be much higher, probably closer to 15%. And someone else—my tenant—has been paying down the mortgage and increasing my equity. This is an example of leveraging, or using other people's money. I made my $10,000 work hard. Although the appreciation isn't spectacular, the investment is still a good one.

During the writing of the first draft for this book, I was considering increasing the leveraging of my $10,000 using the little known tax-saving technique called a 1031 exchange, which was explained earlier in Chapter 12, "Creating a Tax-Favored Environment." As it happened, after doing some calculating, I discovered that it was not to my advantage to trade my $10,000 investment condo in Downers Grove, Illinois for a condo in downtown Chicago.

Not only did I already have a very positive cash flow on the Downers Grove property, my return was very good. Although I did not leverage my $10,000 with a 1031 exchange, I did decide to use leverage and opened a margin account. This type of account is based on the value of your mutual fund, stock/bond portfolio held at a brokerage firm. It allows you to borrow anywhere from 50% to 60% of the portfolio value. The interest rate is quite reasonable and is completely tax-deductible. This action allowed me to purchase, for cash, the downtown condo. Since all of the expenses on rental property are tax-deductible, I was able to create a positive cash flow. Leveraging is a great tool!

An addendum to this story is necessary. Originally I had purchased the second lakefront condo behind my unit, thinking that I would expand by breaking through the common wall, creating a 2,500-square-foot unit. The unit that I newly purchased had been completely remodeled. It contained a fireplace, a Jacuzzi, oak floors and a gorgeous new kitchen. It also has a spectacular east view of the lake. However, as the saying goes, "Man proposes and God disposes." After two tenants who rented this lovely unit "walked"—i.e. left without paying the final month's rent—I decided that the Universe had different plans for me. I sold the second unit, which I had owned for about 1½ years, for $217,000, having paid $187,500 for it. Part of the proceeds is financing the publishing of this book.

Different Methods or Styles of Investing

In addition to employing the investment conventions of dollar-cost averaging, diversification, asset allocation and leveraging, it is also useful to become knowledgeable about the different styles of investing. By combining investment conventions with these methods, you will be adding further diversification to your portfolio and can enhance your success. The US equity market has six distinct styles: Large growth, large value (76%); mid growth and mid value (15%); and small growth and small value (9%). The percentages represent the share of the total market capitalization that each category holds.

THE US STOCK MARKET HAS SIX PRINCIPAL STYLES

Investment styles are related to a company's revenue and future prospects.

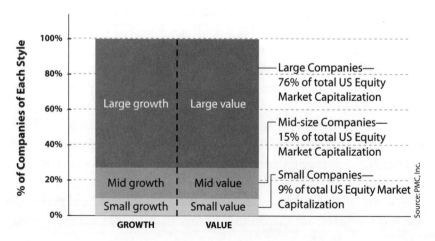

Each style has a distinct fundamental characteristic. Growth stocks often pay small dividends and are priced above the average price/earnings (P/E) (explained later in chapter) because of their expected appreciation. In fact, growth stocks not only have high price-to-earnings, price-to-book (P/B) (explained later in chapter) and high earnings growth, they also have a high beta (are more risky) and a high free cash flow (little debt). On the other hand, value stocks tend to pay higher dividends, have lower P/E and lower P/B ratios, lower betas and more debt.

There is no "best way" to invest at all times. Below is a chart showing how two of the styles—namely, investing in large growth and large value stocks—compared to a non-managed portfolio containing the Standard & Poor's 500 stocks:

STYLES EXHIBIT PERFORMANCE DIFFERENCES IN DIFFERENT YEARS

From 1994 to 1998, there typically has been a substantial difference among the returns of the fundamental styles.

Rates of Return for Some Styles Over Time

YEAR	S & P 500	LARGE VALUE	LARGE GROWTH	STYLE DIFFERENCES
1994	1.3%	-0.6%	3.1%	3.8%
1995	37.6%	37.0%	38.1%	1.1%
1996	23.0%	22.0%	24.0%	2.0%
1997	33.4%	30.0%	36.5%	6.5%
1998	28.6%	14.7%	42.2%	27.5%

Source: PMC, Inc.

Just as no one investment is perfect, there is no one method of investing that is best. Although it might seem that the principles of investment have changed over the years, they have not. In my closing remarks in this book I will remind you that you would be wise to seek out how-to books on investing from any time frame. Some of the older books are just as good or even better than newer ones in helping you understand how to invest. The important thing is to start reading. Let your heart draw you to the right books. I have provided a list of some of my favorites in the Bibliography.

In the same way that some older books are just as good as newer ones, earlier articles from magazines and newspapers can be helpful too. Accordingly, the following is a portion of an article that I wrote a few years ago for the *Daily Record,* a Morristown, New Jersey newspaper. The thoughts are as relevant today as when it was written.

CAPITAL MARKETS OUTLOOK—1996
By Mary F. Ivins, CFP

What is the individual to do given the uncertainties of today's markets? Is hiring professional management worth the money? Or would it be wiser to purchase an unmanaged index of stocks—like Vanguard's S&P 500?

As most of you know, the stock market, as well as the bond market, have given super returns on invested dollars in 1995. Some of the aggressive growth funds have achieved almost a 40% return this year. Will 1996 be more of the same? Maybe not. In 1995, the investor could hardly have gone wrong. Any method of investing, including "chasing performance" was a winner. According to an article published in Morningstar— Mutual Funds, *August 4, 1995, "Recently, at least, **chasing performance** has worked even with newly hatched funds—a strategy not commonly recommended."*

*Since **growth-style investing** has been the winner in the '90s, then it must be the answer to investment success. Well, not really. From 1983- 1988—a period of five years—the typical small cap fund returned just 5% per year, while the S&P compounded at a 20% rate. Morningstar goes on to say, "Shifting market environments do indeed make heroes out of goats, and fools out of geniuses." ". . . a lot of fund investors think they're buying geniuses when they're merely buying long-time growth-stock believers."* [Author's Note: Here, the defining word is "long-time." Since the various styles come in and out of favor, eventually each one will be a winner.]

*Well, if growth-style investing isn't perfect, what is? "**Indexing,**" say the published studies of some finance professors. They . . . suggest that "in contrast with commonly held thought, the average equity fund isn't as good as an unmanaged index, that winning funds probably won't retain their status, and that the best long-term returns don't necessarily accrue to funds following risky, high-growth strategies." While on a risk/reward* *basis, this statement might prove true, during the '90s from a return-only perspective, the index funds have been losers.*

*It is pointed out that during the period 1/90-6/95, the S&P 500, which some of the index funds are patterned after, had an aggregate total return of **82.3%**, while five of the largest, **managed funds returned an average of 103.6%**. The [Morningstar] article further states that, "Simply by spreading their money around, investors would very likely have beaten even the best-performing index."*

*So, if neither growth-style investing nor indexing is the answer, perhaps "**value investing**" is. The theory behind this style is that high-priced stocks get squeezed on two fronts, as earnings come in lower than expected, their price is notched down to match declining expectations. "Meanwhile, the low price/earnings or price/book multiples are prepped to rise on any semblance of good news* (Morningstar—Mutual Funds, *August 4, 1995)." Mario J. Gabelli, the well-known, successful fund manager, believes strongly in **value-style investing**. He chooses stocks ". . . which offer good investment opportunity in a less robust market and places of refuge should the market tide turn." He states, "Going forward, we doubt the market will be as kind to indexers and other non-selective investors."* In support of Gabelli's thinking, the article in Morningstar goes on to say, "But, . . . despite stretches of exceptions, value-driven investment styles do appear to have handily beaten growth styles over the long haul."*

So my advice is to choose stocks and/or mutual funds that have as their focus the different methods of investing. For this, you will have to study the approach of the fund advisors. Even within a type of investing, there are differences in strategies. At any given time, one of the methods will be a winner. Remember to always take an average of your total invested capital. Don't focus on the losers. The losers soon become winners and vice versa. Just diversify and wait.

Remember, don't follow the pack. There are over 6,500 stocks on the exchanges, however only about 1,000 cause the market moves. If you have the desire and commitment, search out the values that are being left on the table by those with the herd mentality.

---

* Even the great fund manager Gabelli doesn't have a crystal ball.

Later I will point out that when you manage your own stock portfolio instead of hiring mutual fund managers to manage parts of your portfolio, you adopt the different styles. This will become clearer in Chapter 15, "Structuring Mutual Fund/Stock and Bond Portfolios," wherein I walk you through how I structured my original portfolio.

- **Have you been using any of the investment conventions mentioned in this chapter?**

- **Do you understand the difference between diversification and asset allocation?**

- **Do you understand why it is "good" if you are dollar-cost averaging and the price of a mutual fund or stock goes lower?**

- **What different styles of investing can you now name?**

CHAPTER

Grasping the Risk/Reward Pyramid

"When it comes to financial risk, one difficulty is that of perception."

DR. CHRISTOPHER L. HAYES, *Money Makeovers*

In this chapter, we will depict the different types of investments in the form of a pyramid. The placement of the investments is meant to show that the higher one goes on the pyramid, the riskier the investment is.

The arrows show that by choosing the investments at the top, your economic benefits will be greater. The real or "perceived" risk will also be greater as you move higher. Notice the word "risk" is sometimes modified by the term "perceived." As stated earlier, even though the stock market seems volatile at times, in any five-year period, investments in stocks have always created real gains. Also keep the following inverse corollary in mind: "The more risk, the more gain."

Hopefully, by examining the potential economic benefits and potential economic constraints of various investments, you will understand the need to move away from fixed investments—such as money markets, CDs, savings accounts and Treasury bills and notes—and into variable investments—such as stock and bond mutual funds and stocks.

A Review of the Statistics Regarding Women & Finances

Unfortunately we, as women, have been taught to choose safety over all else. It is difficult and often painful for us to act in a different manner from that with which we have been socialized. Throughout this book, I have tried to stimulate and inspire you to dream big. The two things in life that motivate us to change are pain and pleasure. Although I prefer to seek out the beauty and pleasure in every situation, perhaps you the reader are more stimulated by the fear of pain.

Therefore I want to remind you of the statistics regarding women and investing, some of which I have mentioned earlier. The first three findings come from OppenheimerFunds, Inc:

1. Only 12% of women who are living and planning with a partner make their own investment decisions,

2. Women are less knowledgeable about investing than men, and

3. Women recognize their lack of knowledge about investing.

Christopher Hayes, Ph.D., of the National Center for Women and Retirement Research, says:

4. 75% of women have their savings in bank accounts.

Joanna L. Krotz, "The Facts of Female Life," January, 1999, issue of *Town & Country* magazine, says:

5. Women start saving later and save less than men,

6. Women earn 74 cents for every dollar men earn (latest US Census Bureau figure is 72 cents),

7. Typically women spend 15% of their working years caring for others,

8. For every year a woman stays at home, she must work five more to recover lost income, pension and career promotion,

7. Only 40% of women receive employer-provided pension benefits,

8. 57% of men have pensions, and

10. Nine out of ten women will be in charge of their own finances for some years.

The US Census Bureau and The National Center for Health add that:

11. About one out of every two marriages ends in divorce,

12. 18%, or 12.2 million women, maintain families alone,

13. Between 1970 and 1994, the number of women living alone doubled from 7 million to 14 million,

14. 73% of women die single,

15. On average, women live seven years longer than men. 52% of women 75 years and over live alone,

16. The average age of widowhood is 56,

17. 80% of widows now living in poverty were not poor before the death of their husband.

The US Bureau of Labor points out that:

18. A 1970 dollar, measured for inflation in the years 1970-1995, was worth 22 cents in 1995.

Hopefully, repetition of many of these statistics has caused you to realize that you really have no choice but to learn how to manage financial assets. Part of acquiring these new skills is learning how to balance the good with the bad. There is no such thing as the perfect investment. There will always be a trade-off.

Weighing Economic Benefits & Constraints

At this point, I'd like to familiarize you with some of the basic potential economic benefits as well as potential economic constraints of various investments. Let's begin by listing the potential economic benefits:

Potential Benefits of Investments

Safety of Principal means that you will receive a dollar back for every dollar that you invest. An example of this type of investment is a bank savings account.

Current Income is usually associated with "fixed-income" investments, such as CDs or bonds. No matter what kind of individual bond you own, there is always a fixed interest rate attached. Years ago, there were coupons that one had to clip and redeem. Currently there are only electronic entries wherein the investor automatically receives his interest payment. Because the interest rate is fixed, there is no uncertainty as to the amount of inflow that you will receive.

If the investor has a need of current income, she/he does not have the option to allow interest to accumulate and compound. However, often the investor receives a check for the interest and then redeposits it into a savings or checking account. Hopefully the reader has learned that this is not a smart move.

Tax Advantages are added when we employ investments that save us tax dollars. Though this is a particularly valuable strategy for those in higher tax brackets, it can also be beneficial for those investors that are in other tax brackets. Oftentimes the taxable equivalent—the return on a taxable investment after taxes are figured in—yields less than the total return—including interest and appreciation—of a non-taxable investment. An example of a income-taxable instrument is a bank account. An example of a tax-advantaged investment is a tax-exempt mutual fund; the interest is tax-free and the appreciation is taxed at the capital gains rate of 20%.

Inflation Hedge means that we must include some growth in our investments, otherwise our investment return will only mirror the economy. For instance, bank-type accounts are usually tied to the current interest rates. Historically these rates have not even kept pace with inflation, especially when taxes are factored in. We are not making any real gains, rather we are standing still—or at times actually going backwards. It is prudent to include inflation in your calculations as to your net return on an investment. An example of an inflation-hedge is an investment in a growth stock.

Potential Constraints of Investments

Loss of Principal means not getting all of your dollars back. An example of this would be selling a bond before maturity if the current interest rates are higher than the coupon interest rate. Another example could be a stock that you are forced to sell in a "down" market for a price lower than what you paid for it.

Loss of Purchasing Power means that your investment return is not keeping pace with inflation.

Non-Liquidity means that you will be penalized for cashing in the investment before the maturity date. An example of this would be a CD.

Market-Timing Loss occurs when you choose or are forced to sell an investment when it is out of favor with the market. This could be a fixed-income investment—a bond—or a variable investment—a stock —or stock or bond mutual fund. At times, even though an investment is said to be "liquid," it still can carry a potential "market timing loss." That is why I have insisted that most of your emergency fund be in dollar-denominated accounts (savings, checking, money markets, or CDs), also known as "cash equivalents."

The old adage that says, "Don't keep all your eggs in one basket" is one to keep in mind. Diversification with appropriate asset allocation, as explained in the last chapter, will prevent you from many of the losses associated with economic constraints while affording you an opportunity to reap large gains from the potential benefits. Again, you are smoothing out the peaks and valleys by employing asset allocation that allows you to average the return for all of your investments.

The Risk/Reward Pyramid

While examining the Risk/Reward Pyramid graphic on the next page, the reader is invited to test her/his ability to name the potential benefits and the potential constraints of each of the investments. As mentioned earlier, you will notice that the higher you go on the pyramid, the more potential reward there is, AND the more real or perceived risk there is. However, if you are ever to achieve your dream of financial independence, you must be willing to step into "the void." You must be willing to take risks.

Now I'll describe each type of investment. Compare your evaluations with the information below. Since most of you are more familiar with the investments at the bottom of the pyramid, we'll start there:

Money Market Funds, Certificates of Deposit (CDs): These are termed cash equivalents. As such, they are really not investments. While the depositor (note the term) is guaranteed that she/he will get all of her/his money back no matter what the economy, often inflation and taxes erode the real return.

Treasury Bills: The government issues these. They are for shorter periods—from 90 days to one year. They usually have a lower coupon (interest) than the long-term bonds. The risk attached to the long-term bond is not there, however there still is risk if interest rates have

RISK/REWARD PYRAMID

Types of Investments

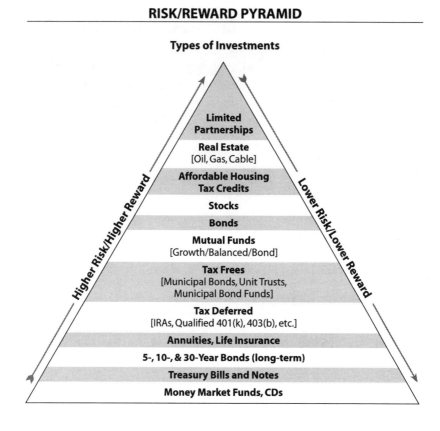

gone up. Also, if interest rates have gone down when the Treasury bill matures, the investor cannot reinvest his proceeds into Treasuries and receive the same interest rate.

5, 10 & 30-Year (long-term) Bonds: The government issues these investments, too. Normally the interest rate for the 5-, 10- or 30-year bonds is slightly higher than that for Treasury bills. This is because in order to be guaranteed your money back, you must hold the bonds for the entire length of maturity and Treasury bills have the shortest maturity. Although the 30-year bonds usually have the highest interest rate and may seem like a "safe" investment, authorities feel that there is quite a bit of risk involved.

A safer investment is in the intermediate (10-year) bond, which historically has returned a minimum of 75% of what the long bond has—with about half of the risk. The risk comes from the fact that the investor might need/want to cash in the bond before the 30-year maturity. If interest rates have risen above the coupon rate on the long-term bond, the investor would receive less than the face value—probably less than she/he paid for it!

Annuities, Life Insurance: These are financial contracts issued by life insurance companies. Since the majority of insurance companies are solvent, they are fairly "safe" investments. In addition, there is a guaranteed death benefit.

Deferred annuities pay out a fixed or a variable payment at some future time. Many of the insurance companies have sophisticated computer systems that allow for periodic distributions, however some of them only allow a lump sum distribution. It would be wise to check into this before committing to buying a company's annuity.

In my opinion, there are a couple of things to be concerned about with investments in annuities. First, if one invests in the accounts guaranteed by the insurance company, one must make certain that the insurance company is quite solvent. There are several agencies, including Standard & Poor's, who rate these companies. Keep in mind that, as with any "fixed" account, the investor will not have inflation protection.

Normally the insurance company hires many mutual fund companies to manage a family of funds for the variable part of an annuity. Presumably the annuitant does not have all of his deposits with one fund manager. However the investor is exposed to the normal risks of market fluctuations.

Although not strictly a risk, the insurance company's penalties can hurt the investor. Should the annuitant want to cancel her/his contract (perhaps to transfer to another insurance company) before the penalty period is over, the initial insurance company recoups its costs by charging as much as a 10% penalty. Of course, there are "no-load"/no-penalty annuity contracts. However, often these do not have the flexibility of the "load" contracts. For instance, some may not allow for periodic distributions, i.e. monthly checks, and the annuity company may not have been in business long enough to learn the best way to run an annuity. Again, do your research and ask questions before you invest.

As I write, I am certain that just the word "insurance" is grating to some of you. Because of my years in that field, I am aware that many people hate insurance. But the use of permanent insurance, such as cash-value life insurance, is still a good planning tool. As the tax law stands today, the insured can take loans out against the cash in her/his life insurance policy and not be taxed on those dollars. The important thing here is to NEVER cash in the policy. To do so would cause immediate recouping of all distributions into one's taxable income.

When we speak of cash-value life insurance, we mean either policies based on a fixed rate of return or on a variable rate of return. This is often confusing to the purchaser. In the fixed-rate insurance, the insurance company guarantees a certain rate of return each year. The way it makes its money is by investing in financial instruments that offer a higher rate than is promised to the insured. Since it invests in volume, it can usually get better returns than the smaller investor can.

However, under present law, insurance companies can only invest a small percentage of their assets in variable investments. Yet variable financial instruments historically have had better returns. Therefore it is often difficult for an insurance company that offers only fixed-rate policies to guarantee a good rate of return.

With a variable life insurance policy, there are no guarantees. In effect, the risk is transferred from the insurance company to the insured —the insurance company is "off the hook." The return that the policyholder receives is based on market returns, not on insurance company guarantees. However I still prefer the variable return policy as it offers better inflation protection. Just as in investing, using a combination of fixed-rate and variable life insurance is the best plan.

Although term insurance is definitely not an investment, I am going to mention it here as we are addressing the subject of life insurance. Term life insurance policies are used to insure for a certain period of time. They can be guaranteed yearly renewable with the premium going up as the insured gets older. Or they can be guaranteed renewable for a certain period of time, say 5, 10, or 20 years. During that time, the premium stays the same for each period. However, at the end of the guaranteed renewable period, the insured must prove that she/he is healthy or insurance-worthy.

Term insurance should not be considered "permanent" insurance, i.e. it should not be purchased as a "life" policy. Only about 2% of term-life policies are ever paid on because when the insured reaches the older ages, the premium becomes exorbitant and often the insured allows the policy to lapse. Again, term insurance is not an investment, however it can be used to purchase protection against the loss of a breadwinner's income while the children are growing into adulthood.

Tax Deferred (IRAs, 401(k) and 403(b) Plans): I have given very good reasons why just about everyone who is eligible should partake fully in these investments. The only risk I see is that often these investments are interest-rate sensitive and don't keep pace with inflation nor provide necessary growth. Since these investments are fully taxed upon distribution, and the investor may not be in a low tax bracket, it would be wise to combine these with "after-tax" investments—like permanent life insurance.

Tax Frees (Municipal Bonds, Unit Trusts, Municipal Bond Funds): In Chapter 12, "Creating a Tax-Favored Environment," and in Chapter 15, "Structuring Mutual Funds/Stock and Bond Portfolios," I discuss these rather fully. The important thing is to combine these types of investments. Each one has advantages and disadvantages. An additional point is that the unit trusts can also be purchased on the stock exchanges. At times these are issued as "original issue," which means that the sponsor often sells them without a sales charge. I have used these for my parents' portfolio with good results.

Mutual Funds (Growth/Balanced/Bond): The risk here is mostly "market risk." That is, if you choose or need to cash in the mutual fund when the stock market is low or interest rates are high, you may suffer a loss. This is why I have stressed that these investments are not short-term. Presumably, even if you need to get at the cash after your investments have been held for a minimum of five years, they will have appreciated. Therefore you won't suffer any loss.

Stocks and Bonds: These investments are for the sophisticated investor. Again, unless you can afford at least $10,000-$20,000 to structure a diversified stock/bond portfolio, stick with mutual funds.

Affordable Housing Tax Credits: Although I have placed these near the top of the pyramid because the SEC considers them "limited partnerships," I highly recommend the use of this little-known and legal way to reduce your taxes. The only risk, as I see it, is that your investment advisor is not sufficiently sophisticated to explain them fully.

Limited Partnerships (Real Estate—REITs, Oil and Gas, Cable): The only limited partnership that I would recommend is a REIT. These are sold on the exchanges. A REIT is a bundle of real estate investments, usually commercial, that a syndicator puts together. By law, the REIT is required to pay out 90% of all of its profits to the limited partners. Quite often, this is a better interest rate than an investor can find in other fixed-income vehicles. In addition, since the underlying investment is in real estate, the investor, i.e. limited partner, stands to gain if the value of the real estate goes up. Again, this is a method of diversifying into real estate.

A word about the term "limited partner." A limited partner is one who is only responsible for her/his investment. In other words, the general partner, the syndicator, would be the person/s sued if anything should go wrong with the partnership.

Now that you have a better idea of how each investment listed on the Risk/Reward Pyramid functions, as well as how inflation and taxes impact on your investment results, you are ready to take the Risk Tolerance Questionnaire on the next page.

Risk Tolerance Questionnaire

To help you evaluate your possible comfort level with various degrees of risk, I have provided the following sample Risk Tolerance Questionnaire. There are many of these questionnaires available—some more sophisticated than others. When you work with an investment advisor, she/he will ask you to complete the one that is being used by her/his company. Just as in the other questionnaires used throughout this book, go with your feeling in choosing an answer.

If your answers were in the lower range, you must start taking more risks in your investments. You can begin by taking small risks, such as putting a portion of your investment dollar into growth-type investments. As pointed out earlier, fixed investments including bonds (represented by the lower numbers on the Risk Tolerance Questionnaire) often will not earn a positive return when inflation and taxes are considered. AND cash equivalents—like money markets, CDs and savings/checking accounts—are not investments.

If your answer for #1 was 5, you are "in the money." In the next chapter, I share how my original investment of $5,700 in a growth-type investment, AIG, is now valued at over $180,000.

RISK TOLERANCE QUESTIONNAIRE

	STRONGLY DISAGREE				STRONGLY AGREE
I prefer growth-type investments to income-type (dividends and interest).	1	2	3	4	5
I want my investments to outpace inflation even if I risk not getting all of my money back.	1	2	3	4	5
I understand that equity-type investments go up and down frequently. I can accept this risk in exchange for a possible higher long-term gain.	1	2	3	4	5
Obtaining above average returns means accepting above-average risk.	1	2	3	4	5

More food for thought:

A LOOK AT LONG-TERM RETURNS

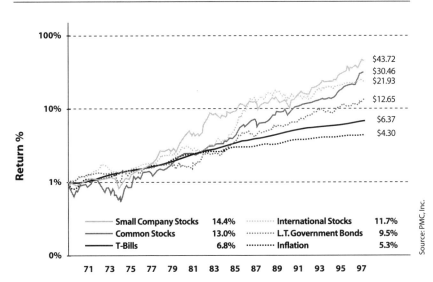

Small Company Stocks	14.4%	International Stocks	11.7%
Common Stocks	13.0%	L.T. Government Bonds	9.5%
T-Bills	6.8%	Inflation	5.3%

Source: PMC, Inc.

Note: Inflation averaged 5.3%. In other words, it took $4.30 to purchase $1.00 of goods and services in 1997. A dollar in each representative investment was worth in 1997: T-Bills, $6.37; long-term gov-

179

ernment bonds, \$12.65; international stocks, \$21.93, US common stocks, \$30.46; and US small company stocks, \$43.72.

The Big Picture

At the end of this chapter is a checklist for you to use in determining how well you are doing in taking control of your financial destiny. The **Checklist for Your Personal Finances** covers many aspects of financial planning, and will help you see how your investments fit into the big picture of money management.

Unfortunately I did not have the room or the time to address all the wealth preservation issues (estate planning) addressed in the **Checklist for Your Personal Finances.** Perhaps in a subsequent book, I will do that. In the meantime, you can gather information on wealth preservation from other sources. I have included my favorites in the Bibliography along with titles to assist you in growing spiritually and emotionally.

- **Do you now better understand how willing you are to take on risk?**

- **How much of your investment portfolio is in growth-type investments?**

- **Do you understand the importance of including a variety of asset classes in your investments?**

- **Do you understand the term "real gain?" (Hint: Relates to taxes and inflation.)**

- **What is market risk? (Hint: See above under Investment Constraints.)**

- **What is liquidity risk?**

- **What is risk of loss of principal?**

- **What is loss of purchasing power risk?**

- **Are there some areas that the checklist for your personal finances pointed out that need your attention?**

CHECKLIST FOR YOUR PERSONAL FINANCES

YES   NO

Spending and Saving

☐ ☐ Would you need to borrow to pay bills if you became ill or lost your job?

☐ ☐ Do you pay yourself first and have a systematic savings plan?

☐ ☐ Do you have an emergency fund in cash equivalents to cover three to six months of living expenses?

☐ ☐ Do you owe more than 15% of your take-home pay to bills, excluding mortgage, rent and car payments?

Investments

☐ ☐ Are your investments prudently diversified? Do they contain stock and bond mutual funds?

☐ ☐ Do you have a well-defined investment policy?

☐ ☐ If you own stock-type investments, do you accept the fluctuations in their value?

☐ ☐ If you own fixed-income securities, do you understand the interest rate risk, i.e., when rates go up, the value of your investment goes down?

☐ ☐ Do you use a reliable, (read *honest*) source of investment advice, i.e. a good broker or a personal financial planner?

Insurance

☐ ☐ Is your home insured for today's replacement cost?

☐ ☐ Are you certain that you would receive 100% replacement costs for any personal items destroyed in a fire?

☐ ☐ Do you know the limits for theft on your silver, furs, collectibles and guns?

☐ ☐ Is your auto liability sufficient? Do you understand that the amount for un/under-insured is the amount you would receive to cover your or your passenger's medical costs?

☐ ☐ If you are healthy, are you raising your deductible on your medical policy?

☐ ☐ Do you know who would pay the bills if you were unable to work? Are you covered for long-term disability?

☐ ☐ Do you understand the differences in insurance policies? Are you being realistic about the amount of life insurance you or your spouse needs? Did you know that you can "minimum-pay" your present policies, i.e., let the dividends and accumulated values pay the policy off?

Continued on next page

Taxes

☐ ☐ Did you receive more than 5% of your taxes back in the form of a refund? Did you know that you are giving the government an interest-free loan? To avoid this, increase the number of exemptions on your W-4.

☐ ☐ Are you aware of the ways to reduce your taxes by reducing your marginal tax bracket? Take a look at any income other than your employment income.

☐ ☐ Are you using tax-saving techniques? Learn about tax-exempts, IRAs and qualified employer retirement plans, annuities and tax credit programs. Are you taking advantage of itemizing your deductions?

☐ ☐ Did you know that the highest federal tax bracket is 36.9% and that the current Social Security FICA tax is 15.3% for employees (6.2% + 1.45% paid by employee and 7.65% paid by employer) and 15.3% for self-employed individuals?

☐ ☐ Are you accumulating wealth tax-deferred and/or tax-free? Or even better through the use of tax credits which offset your taxes dollar for dollar?

Retirement

☐ ☐ Are you planning for a dignified and fun retirement?

☐ ☐ Do you think Social Security will be around when you retire?

☐ ☐ Do you realize that you will need to invest in inflation-proof investments even during retirement?

☐ ☐ Did you use the Retirement Income Worksheet to determine how much of a "nest egg" you will need? What is your desired lifestyle during retirement?

Estate Planning

☐ ☐ Do you and other adult members of your family have wills?

☐ ☐ Are you aware that in 1998 the government passed new limits for personal estate tax exemptions? In 1999, the exemption is $650,000. This amount will increase by $50,000 annually until it reaches the amount of $750,000.

☐ ☐ Is your total estate over the personal exemption amount? If married, have you incorporated a by-pass trust in your wills wherein the first person to die has her/his amount of exemption placed in a trust in order that it won't be passed on and be exposed to estate taxes in the second estate?

☐ ☐ Do you have general powers of attorney for you and your spouse and for one other family member?

☐ ☐ Do you know where your important papers are? Have you told the individual with your unlimited or general power of attorney where they are?

☐ ☐ Are your living wills and medical directives in keeping with the changes in your state's tax law?

Structuring Mutual Fund/ Stock and Bond Portfolios

"Reading this book and obtaining knowledge is good BUT IT IS NOT GOOD ENOUGH. Personal finance is 80% behavior and only 20% knowledge."

DAVE RAMSEY, *More Than Enough*

We learn by doing. Hopefully you can join an investment club that will assist you in learning the principles of investing. There you can learn without feeling threatened. A common feature of these clubs is having only women members. (According to the National Association of Investors Corporation, more than 60% of investment club members are women.) One thing that you are likely to master is how to use dividend reinvestment plans (DRPs), as this way of investing is quite often recommended by investment clubs.

Having an individual or a group to share your knowledge with is beneficial. Years ago, when I was first learning, I had no one to talk to about my investments. I still laugh when I recall visiting a library in the small town of New Albany, Indiana. I was working in the town at the time for a Snelling and Snelling office. I entered the library and asked for the copy of *Value Line*. The librarian stated that it was already being used. I located the man who was looking at the large binder. I inquired if he invested, as I was hungry for someone to exchange ideas with. He reacted as though I was coming on to him.

Mutual Funds

I started my investment history with investments in stocks. But if you do not want to devote the necessary time and energy to do the research on stocks or feel unsure of your ability, start by choosing mutual funds. The important thing is to take action. It is not enough to just to read about investing. Start small; invest in mutual funds until you are able to assume more risk.

Mutual funds have several advantages. As mentioned earlier, a mutual fund is made up of a bundle of stocks, bonds or both, plus some cash equivalents. This offers the extra safety of diversification. Another advantage is having an expert to manage the funds. If the mutual fund manager does not produce an above average return for the investor, she/he is removed. Each fund is usually designed to achieve a different objective. When the mutual fund industry was first started about 20 years ago, it was easier to determine the focus of the individual funds. Now, because of the popularity of this means of investing, there are over 11,000 mutual funds to choose from—more mutual funds than stocks on all of the exchanges.

Although the number of mutual funds is huge, by carefully reading the prospectus (pamphlet describing the fund), you can usually figure out what the fund's aim is. It will state that it is primarily interested in "growth," "dividend growth," "income," etc. Just be certain that a fund that calls itself a "balanced fund" actually holds stocks and bonds in a somewhat equal proportion. While a balanced fund is a rather conservative investment, recently a fund that claimed to be "balanced" actually held high yield bonds and small growth stocks—neither of which is considered "conservative." Also, the prospectus should have a listing of the featured industries and the percentage of the portfolio in each industry. And under the industries, there should be a listing of the current holdings/companies in the portfolio.

Studying the information on the fund's portfolio is a good method to learn how portfolios are constructed. In addition, the prospectuses will also tell you how often the individual stocks in the fund are traded. Naturally the holdings will change, however, in my opinion, it is best to choose a manager that does not turn over the portfolio too often. After all, whenever the manager takes capital gains, you must pay taxes on it. Also, abundant trading can add to the cost of managing the fund.

If the prospectus that you receive does not have this information, it is a "partial prospectus." Ask for a complete prospectus.

Another way to choose the correct mutual fund is to look it up in the library—Lipper Analytical, Morningstar or Value Line Mutual Fund. Or, find an advisor who has access to "Fund Analysis," which gives information on specific funds like the one exhibited below:

ANALYSIS OF A SPECIFIC FUND

Manager Information		General Information	
Capital Research & Management		Fund founded	1958
		Prospectus date	11-01-1998
Los Angeles, CA		Min initial invest	$1,000
(310)996-6000		Rear load	1.000%
(800)421-9900		Expense ratio	0.700%
		12b-1 fee	0.240%
		Max sales charge	5.750%

Performance as of 1Q1999

	Qtr	1 Year	3 Year	5 Year	StdDev	Beta
Growth Fund of America	6.0%	25.0%	25.4%	22.1%	17.9%	1.06
S & P 500 Index	5.0%	18.5%	28.1%	26.2%	15.5%	1.00
Lehman Govt/Corp Index	-1.2%	6.5%	7.8%	7.7%	3.7%	-0.06
Salomon T-Bills 3 Month	1.1%	4.9%	5.1%	5.2%	0.1%	0.00
Avg. of Growth Funds	2.6%	8.0%	19.8%	18.9%	17.6%	1.11

Avg. Composition (Last 60 months)

Bonds 91%
9%
Stocks

Asset Class Analysis (Last 60 months)

LC SC PB EU EM HQ HY IB CE RE

The chart is for the Growth Fund of America. It is one of the superior funds managed by Capital Research & Management, California. The name of the fund is stated at the top. The performance of the fund is compared to several indices; however, the most important one is the comparison between it and other growth funds.

Looking at the chart, we see that this fund has done very well in all periods from the current quarter to 5 years. Looking at the comparison for "standard deviation," which is the measure of the fund's volatility, we see that it is about average for growth funds. However, its beta (see glossary) is lower than the average growth fund. This is important because a fund that has wide swings in its year-to-year values actually earns less for the investor.

This is a "load" fund (see glossary), which means that it has a sales charge. By studying the report, we see that the maximum sales charge is 5.75%. Unlike many other mutual fund managers, Capital Research & Management feels that the investor is best served by offering only front-end load funds. Although the report also lists a "back-end" load, I called the company and was told that that there used to be a charge levied for qualified-plan contributors who terminated within one year. Currently, there is no sales charge for those who use Capital Research & Management to manage their qualified plans.

Notice that the expense ratio is less than 1%. This is good. And, the 12 b-1 fee is very small, 0.24%. The chart below this information gives the type of assets held in the fund over the past year. Notice that the fund contains mostly the asset class of stocks. How this class is diversified is in the chart to the right. Because of space limitations, abbreviations are used, e.g. LC = large capitalization and SC = small caps. The small percentage held in bonds is also shown. This will give you some idea of what to look for when choosing a mutual fund. Again, don't be afraid of paying a one-time sales charge for a superior fund and the valuable knowledge of the investment advisor. The above fund's 5.75% sales charge spread over a holding period of the minimum of five years is negligible. And, the value is there.

By signing up for $50 a month, you can own this fund. Or, if you prefer, you can open an account with $1,000, the minimum. There are many funds that will allow you to get involved for $25 a month and have lower minimums. With as little as $100 a month, you can start a nice portfolio that combines all of the investment strategies mentioned above. All of this can be done automatically. AND, this is the preferred method, because once it's set up, usually the investor doesn't pay too much attention to it—or its results.

Many of you are already familiar with this concept because of the proliferation of the 401(k) plans. Hopefully you are not among the majority who wrongly invest in the fixed-income-type funds. Inside or outside of the 401(k), you can create a diversified portfolio using mutual funds. If you are investing on your own, start with $100 a month and choose to put $25 into each of four diversified mutual funds. For instance, you might have:

1. A large-company growth fund that mostly holds stocks in the large capitalization corporations—the blue-chip companies like Coca Cola;

2. A small capitalization stock fund that would hold companies with less than $6,000,000 in capitalization. (Capitalization is the stock price times the number of stockholders.) These would be non-dividend paying and a "pure" growth play;

3. A high yield bond fund, which holds inferior grade bonds—rated BB and B. This type of investment is perceived to be risky, but out-performed all fixed income investments and broke even with the return on equities in the period from 1980-1994.

4. An international fund. Here, if you can find one that focuses on the established/middle-capitalized companies, you would not be as exposed to the volatility of the "emerging markets." But, smaller companies usually have greater growth.

If you can only afford three funds, use a "balanced fund" in place of the large capitalization growth (1, above) and the bond fund (3). A balanced fund will offer some protection from the volatility of the market. The reason for this is that there is usually a direct corollary between how these asset classes perform (i.e. when bonds go up, stocks go down and vice versa). Later, after each of your funds has reached, say, $3,000, you can diversify further. Diversification is still the name of the game.

However, don't get too diversified, using funds that mirror one another. For instance, you may prefer to choose mutual funds that are oriented toward growth. Choose managers with the same goals but with differing strategies. If you are going to duplicate the focus of the funds in this way, be certain that the styles of the managers are not the same.

On the next page is a graph showing some sample portfolios. A is the most conservative; E is for the person who has a high-risk tolerance.

You must determine your comfort level regarding risk-taking. Taking risk-tolerance questionnaires, such as the one provided in Chapter 14, will be of some value. However, hopefully, after reading the information I've shared with you, you won't keep such a large amount of cash equivalents in your portfolio. Cash equivalents (CDs, savings accounts, money markets, etc.) are not much of an investment; they are more of a place to "park" money while waiting for the right opportunity.

The secret is to continually invest. No one has a crystal ball. Perfect "market timing"—i.e. buying stocks when they are low and selling

GLOBAL PORTFOLIOS THAT MEET A RANGE OF OBJECTIVES

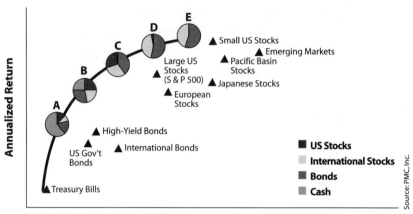

them when they are high every time you invest is impossible. Statistically, those who accumulate wealth do so by buying, diversifying and holding their investments for a long time. If you are using mutual funds, let the manager manage them. In stocks, as long as the fundamentals are good do nothing. In fact, as mentioned earlier, buy more of the same stock. Statistically, the individual investor has not done as well as one who pays for investment management. On the next page is a graph to illustrate this point:

Note: The reason, I suspect, that the professionally guided investor does better is that having paid for advice or a sales commission/load, she/he is reluctant to cash in the investment when the market goes down. In fact, this study by Dalbar, an internationally known investment research firm, found that the average holding period for a "no-load" fund was 18 months versus 4.2 years for a "load" fund. Clearly, 18 months is not long enough to determine how an investment is going to react in different markets. So even if you choose to work directly with a "no-load" company, diversify and hold on.

When choosing your funds, here are the things to watch for:

- The length of life for the fund—at least five years. This means that the fund has been in existence at least five years.

PROFESSIONAL ADVICE MAY HAVE AN ADVANTAGE

Sales force-advised investors outperformed the average investor during the period from January, 1984, to December, 1995.

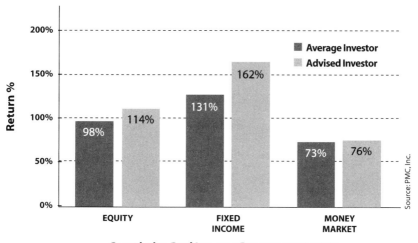

Cumulative Real Investor Returns 1984-1995

- Continuity of management—not less than five years under same manager.

- The fund is what it says it is. It does not call itself a "balanced fund" (one holding large growth stocks and bonds) but then is really made up of 50% high yield bonds and 50% aggressive small capitalization stocks.

- The past history is impressive—at least in the top 25% for the last five years. Lipper Analytic Services publications, which you can find at the library, will be good resources for this determination.

If you were fortunate to receive a large inheritance and would like to hire a professional money management company, I would suggest looking into firms who do nothing but manage financial assets. Unfortunately, in my opinion, many financial planners have assumed the role of money managers. Having operated my own financial planning firm, I realize that much of the financial planner's time is used for other responsibilities that take attention away from watching the markets. Therefore

189

I personally do not feel comfortable with the idea of referring to myself as a money manager, whose only job is to watch the market.

In this book, I have included some statistics that were contained on slides provided by a particular money management company that I work with. Again, I believe in diversification and only place a portion of my client's money with this firm. This type of management is not for everyone. Professional money managers require a minimum level of investment—usually $100,000. This amount makes sense to me since the management fees on a smaller amount would eat up the profits.

The company I am referring to is called PMC, Inc. or Professional Management Consultants, Inc. They bought Adam Investing, which was the original company that I worked with. I am told that PMC, Inc. will continue to actively manage the Adam accounts in a very similar way.

If you are looking for specific mutual funds to invest in, you might consider those illustrated in the following graph. At the time of this writing, the funds mentioned were rated as superior. They also adhere to the criteria for choosing mutual funds as explained above. This graph shows both asset allocation and fund allocation within a sample portfolio.

This sample portfolio allocation will give you some idea of how to choose funds within your asset allocation. I'm not certain if high yield bonds were used in the bond portion; however, these bonds react differently than regular bonds. They act more like stocks, whose underlying value is increased as the stock market goes up.

PRECISE ASSET ALLOCATION USING SUPERIOR MUTUAL FUNDS

Sample Portfolio

Asset Allocation pie chart:
- Bonds 28%
- Money Markets 1%
- Large US 32%
- Small US 12%
- International 27%

Fund Allocation pie chart:
- PIMCO Total Return 19%
- Price Int'l Bond 7%
- William Blair Growth 14%
- MAS Value 21%
- Mutual Beacon 14%
- Warburg Pincus Int'l 25%

Source: PMC, Inc.

Asset Allocation   **Fund Allocation**

It is only recently that I have come to understand high yield bonds. Because companies that might have a lower Standard & Poor's rating issue the bonds, they must offer a higher interest rate to attract buyers for their bonds (debt). The reason for the lower rating could be that the company has only been in existence a short time or possibly it has a lot of debt.

Although these bonds are rated lower, historically they have provided excellent returns. In fact, using them adds safety to the fixed-income (bond) portion of your portfolio. While volatile stock prices hurt these bonds, the yields do not fall as far as with Treasury bonds. It is wise to remember that yields go down for bonds when their prices rise. Now I regularly recommend using high yield bond funds in my clients' portfolios.

In Chapter 14, "Grasping the Risk/Reward Pyramid," we looked at some investment constraints. It is very beneficial to be aware of the trade-offs between investments. All investments carry some form of risk. Often women only see volatility as a risk. Hopefully, after absorbing the last chapter, you now better understand all the meanings of risk.

Stock Portfolios

My investment strategy has not changed over the years. After I received my final divorce settlement of $20,000 from my first marriage, I used about $10,000 to purchase five stocks that I had carefully researched. In this research, I included my constant reading of financial material as well as the *Value Line* reports. I not only diversified by industry, size of company, and stock exchange, but I also diversified by my style of investing.

It was at this time, 1979, that I became acquainted with the financial magazine, *Forbes*. Since that time, I have been a continual subscriber. Much of my investment success can be attributed to the information I find in this magazine. One of the stocks mentioned in *Forbes* was Analog Devices, a manufacturer of analog signaling equipment that is used to convert analog signals to digital. I think that it was mentioned in the "Up and Comers" section. At any rate, I decided to buy 100 shares of this company. This was to be a representative investment in a small growth stock. It contained the following features: (1) It was a technology company, (2) It was also a small capitalization growth company, (3) Its stock was offered on the OTC stock exchange, and (4) Its purchase reflected growth-style investing.

As previously pointed out, I bought 100 shares—a round lot—at $21 a share, which, historically, was the highest paid for the stock. A few months later, the price had gone down to $15.75. And although "on paper" I had lost about 25% of my investment, I decided to purchase another 100 shares. Again, there is no real loss until an investment is sold. Now my average cost per share was $18.375. As stated earlier, this number is derived by adding together the cost of my two investments, $2,100 and $1,575 = $3,675 and dividing by my new number of shares, 200 = $18.375 per share. "Averaging down" was explained earlier, too; however it is a very effective way to be successful and bears repeating.

I felt comfortable purchasing the additional 100 shares because of the information in the 10-K Analog Devices had sent me. I already mentioned the 10-K form, which each company must file annually with the Securities and Exchange Commission (SEC). In it, the corporation states its method of doing business and any new focuses for the company. After reading the mission statement and the information on the background of the officers of the corporation, I was impressed with both the integrity of the company and the caliber of its officers.

Although Analog Devices' stock languished during the 1980s, as did most small capitalization stocks, I continued to believe in the company's fundamentals and did not sell my holding. At times it is difficult to hold on to a stock that has gone down in price and does not pay dividends. Analog, like most high-tech growth companies, finances its expansion from within and doesn't pay out its profits in dividends. Instead of dividends, the growth companies usually give their investors more shares through "stock splits." Usually, these are "two for one" (2/1), which means that for every share that you own, you receive an additional share.

Today Analog has carved out a nice niche, specializing in the manufacture of a specific kind of computer chip. Quite recently it made a deal with the largest computer-chip maker in the world, Intel. My original number of shares has grown to almost 3,000 through Analog Devices stock splits. In spite of the fact that I sold some of the shares and took some profits—about $12,000—my original $3,600 investment in Analog Devices is currently valued at around $90,000.

The purpose of sharing this story is not to brag. Rather, it is to drive home the point that you must believe in yourself. Had I been faint of heart, when my investment in Analog Devices lost over 25% of its value in such a short time I would have sold instead of purchasing another 100 shares. Had I not researched the company and felt that the market was not pricing this stock correctly, I most certainly would have sold. This is a lesson in making a decision based on deep research and believing in inner self and having patience. This is called taking a calculated risk.

Please pay attention to the idea of "calculated risk-taking." My investment in Analog Devices was exactly that. When I invested, Analog was a relatively new company, perhaps five years old. Its stock was traded on the NASDAQ. This is an organization owned by the NASD (National Association of Security Dealers) for the purpose of providing a computerized system for stock price quotations of smaller stocks. At times it is referred to as the "over the counter" market. The NASDAQ has grown tremendously since 1979. However, at that time, it was not considered to be as safe as the NYSE (New York Stock Exchange). About a year after I purchased the stock, Analog's officers qualified the company and placed it on the "big board" or NYSE.

I still have most of the stocks that I purchased around that time. All have done well. As I have already stated, I have taken profits in Analog Devices of probably around $12,000. In fact, early on, I sold enough of the stock in my original portfolio to recoup all of the money that I had invested. Therefore, my "cost basis" (cost of ownership) is "0." Although the first number in the following list is what I invested, I actually have nothing invested at this time.

The second number listed is what the investment is approximately valued at today—stock prices fluctuate daily. $1,500 in Golden West Financial, $60,000; $1,800 in General Datacomm, $1,300; $1,500 in Gulf & Western, a.k.a. Paramount Communications, now Viacom, Inc.,$12,000, (*Note:* when Viacom bought out Paramount with cash and stock, in addition to Viacom's stock, I received about $12, 000); and $3,600 in Parker Hannifin, $25,000. (Note: I also took profits in Parker Hannifin, probably close to $12,000.) This may all seem confusing; however, the important thing is that I did not experience any losses in my original portfolio. In fact, I have made spectacular gains.

But, over the years, I have had a few—very few—losers. One of them was a computer company that manufactured mega or very large computers. If memory serves me correctly, it went bankrupt and I was able to write off my losses for income tax purposes. I tell this story because it illustrates my belief that "what goes around comes around." I had bought this stock on the recommendation of a "would be" client. I use the term "would be" because although I had done a lot of work for this man, he bought insurance from someone else. To me this reflects on his honesty. Therefore, it was no wonder that both he and his company later suffered.

Also, it should be noted that General Datacomm Industries, Inc. is not doing well. Its stock is probably selling at its all-time low of about $3.31 a share. But I continue to hold it for three reasons: (1) I have a "0" cost basis, (2) This holding does not represent much in terms of my total portfolio, and (3) I still believe that it will turn itself around or be bought out. Again, we need not focus on our so-called "losers." In life, we do not expect to bat 1,000. In a similar way, it is the over-all picture that we should focus on in investing.

I probably kept about $5,000 of the remaining $10,000 from the final divorce settlement in liquid money—in a bank account—and bought more stock at a later date with the other $5,000. An important point to keep in mind is that you would be wise never to put more than about $10,000 into the market at one time. Even if you have a large inheritance, keep most of it in a money-market fund and put it into the market in increments.

This is especially important advice if the stock market is "frothy." This is a term used when the P/Es (Price to Earnings ratio) or P/Bs (Price to Book ratio) are historically high. The P/E has to do with what the market thinks of a stock, i.e., how it prices it and the real number of the company's past earnings. It is stated as a percentage, the "P" stands for price and the "E" stands for earnings. The number for earnings comes from dividing the company's net profits—after deducting for expenses and taxes—by the number of share-holders.

Look in the financial section of the newspaper. You will notice that as of this writing Coca-Cola (on the NYSE) is selling at a P/E of 46. This means that it is selling for 46 times each dollar of earnings. This is a very high P/E. Contrast that with the P/E for American International Group (AIG), also sold on the NYSE, at 22. This stock is selling at 22 times earnings. As pointed out earlier, growth stocks— like Coca-Cola—command a higher P/E. However, AIG historically has been a tremendous growth stock, but it seems that the market does not classify it as such.

The book value, or the "B" in the P/B ratio, represents the amount of money each shareholder would receive if all of the tangible or hard assets of the company were sold. Quite often the market is not valuing the stock highly enough. This is especially so as the book value is based on the tangible assets—e.g. the factory, inventories, etc. The company's intangible assets—e.g. name recognition, reputation of the company, etc.— are not included in the Book Value. Again, the "P" in P/B stands for "Price."

Investing in the stock market is exciting. However, having said that, I caution you against putting money into the stock or bond market that you need for your emergency fund. Furthermore, unless you have at least $10,000, preferably $20,000, and can diversify into at least four well-chosen stocks, use mutual funds. And if you do purchase stocks, if at all possible, buy the stocks of an industry that you are familiar with.

Try to find good values, i.e., where the market has seemingly undervalued the stock that is selling at a low P/E and/or low P/B. *Hint: Value Line* gives a complete list of these types of stocks each month. In fact, *Value Line* has a third list, "Free Cash Flow," which is a measurement of the companies' cash flow with depreciation and amortization added back—remember, they are only "book" entries and do not represent actual cash that was used in operations. " If you find a stock listed on all of these lists, buy it.

Purchasing stocks with low P/Es and low P/Bs is known as "value investing." This type of investing was favored by past investment giants like Benjamin Graham and current ones like Warren Buffet. In the above example, if I had a choice between buying Coca-Cola and American International Group, I would definitely buy AIG. It is selling for a more normal market P/E, which is still above the historical average of 17-18, but much lower than the current P/E for the S&P Index of 36-38, and it is a superior stock.

AIG was the stock that I was researching back in 1979 at the New Albany Library. Eventually I was able to use the *Value Line* reports. I looked up the company that I had read about in one of the financial publications that I read daily. The report in *Value Line* was very favorable and contained a graph showing that American International Group's (AIG's) profits had continually grown at more than 15% annually. Looking back, this had to be spectacular in the recession of the late 1970s. Even then, the price of the stock was $67, which was much higher than I was used to paying. I didn't feel comfortable buying 100 shares, so instead I bought 30. Later I rounded my holdings up to 100 by purchasing another 70. This probably was in 1979 or 1980. Today my original 100 shares have grown to 1,579 through stock splits and are valued at approximately $180,000.

Again, this is a growth play; the company pays .190% in dividends. However, as pointed out earlier, it can also be a value play. Since my original investment in AIG, I have learned much more about the company. It is an insurance company that specializes in marketing its offerings to the Pacific Basin countries. In fact, approximately 35% of its profits come from this part of the world. Recently the economies of these countries have suffered tremendous losses. However, AIG and its stock have not been hurt. Perhaps the market realizes, as I do, that AIG has operated in the Pacific Basin since 1933. Undoubtedly, it is busy buying shares in the well-managed companies that were dumped along with the poorly managed companies by nervous investors.

This is an important lesson. As usually happens, investors overreact on bad news. As of this writing, I am advising my clients to buy funds that specialize in the Pacific Basin. Since the price of the shares of the Asia-Pacific mutual funds has dropped considerably, I am certain that the managers of these funds are buying up the shares of the well-managed companies, too.

And if my clients feel comfortable with the current price of AIG, which is around $117 a share, I am encouraging them to purchase it. Again, this story is told for a reason. Don't be fearful of buying a stock that seems expensive. Examine the track record of the company. Although past profitability does not always tell the entire story, it is still a good barometer. Just as in our personal lives, "success breeds success." This is true because a successful pattern has been established.

Bond Portfolios

Although I do not have much personal experience in structuring bond portfolios, the following is valuable information. In Chapter 12, "Creating a Favorable Tax Environment," we discussed purchasing individual bonds; however, just as with building a stock portfolio, diversification is of the utmost importance. Therefore, if you don't have enough money to invest in several bonds, thus spreading your risk, it probably would be wiser to invest in what are termed "unit trusts." These are put together by issuers, e.g. Nuveen, and usually include around 20 different bonds. These bonds will carry a variety of ratings, however usually not below the investment-grade of BBB. The bonds will also have different maturities.

In the case single bonds or bond unit trusts, you will pay some commission. Individual bonds are marked up from 1 point (1%) to 3 points (3%) depending on what the market will bear. Unit trusts carry a one-time front-end commission of 3%, however there is no cost to sell the unit trust, and the issuer usually provides an active secondary market. And because the bonds within the unit trust are not actively traded, the service charge is quite low. Furthermore, you can buy an "insured trust," which guarantees that you will get all of your money—both interest payments and principal—should any of the bonds be defaulted. However, please be aware that the incidence of municipal bonds defaulting historically has been minuscule, and you will give up at least .5%, usually 1%, for this benefit.

It also may be mentioned that a system of investing to protect one's assets in individual bonds—taxable or tax free—is called "laddering." In "laddering," one purchases bonds with different maturities. In that manner, should interest rates go up, the bonds with the longest maturity will be the ones mostly affected; while the bonds with the shorter maturities will be affected less. This is so because the longer that the maturity is, the longer you will have to wait to get your principal back. As mentioned earlier, some experts feel that intermediate bonds—those with a 10-year maturity—are the best. They cite that one is able to receive about 75% of the average return without the risk of losing big in the case of a long-term bond.

Note: When interest rates move up or down, the price of a bond typically moves in the opposite direction. Here is an example of what this could mean:

> **Example** **Assumptions: $10,000 AAA, 20-year bond, coupon = 6%. You have owned this bond for 10 years and you must sell it before the 20-year maturity.**
> Because the current interest rate on a 20-year bond is lower than 6%, you would make a profit. A new buyer would have to pay a premium, i.e. more than $10,000. However, even though the new owner is receiving the coupon rate of 6%, she/he had to pay more than the $10,000; therefore the return is less than 6%. To find out the exact return, divide the normal income of $600 by the amount of the investment, $10,500. You will find that the return is 5.7%.

The above example is meant to illustrate that even the bond market has some risk. If the new bond holder were forced to sell, she/he might not receive the full $10,500. We have examined risk/reward in Chapter 14, "Grasping the Risk/Reward Pyramid." While historically bonds have protected the investor's purchasing power, i.e. kept pace with inflation, the growth needed to make substantial gains in one's portfolio has been in the stock market.

Other types of bonds can also be purchased in a mutual fund. Here we are only examining tax-free bond mutual funds. In addition to purchasing tax-free bonds individually or in unit trusts, you can also purchase them in the form of mutual funds. The single bond or the bundle of bonds in a unit trust is a "closed-end" investment, that is, there is no further buying and selling. What you have is what you have. The difference in an "open-end" tax-free mutual fund is that the manager is able to alter the mix of his portfolio depending on where she/he feels that interest rates are headed.

While this ability to alter the mix protects the investor somewhat from the fluctuations in pricing due to severe swings in current interest rates, normally the management charge is higher. Unlike the "passive" management in unit trusts and the "no" management in individual bonds, these accounts are "actively" managed. In addition to the higher management charge, the investor may incur a higher commission charge at the time of purchase.

Again it is not always the cheapest way that will bring you the greatest reward. My advice to my clients is to not look at what's going in but rather look at what's coming out. I once compared a "no-load" tax-free mutual fund against a 4% front-end-load tax-free mutual fund. Using the history of the two funds, I was able to show my client that even with the one-time 4% load, he would have received about $3,000 more in the load fund if it were held for 10 years. As this was a "closed-minded" person, he chose to purchase a "no-load" fund.

- **Have you read a mutual fund prospectus?**
- **Do you understand the difference between a partial prospectus and a complete one?**
- **What do you need to have before investing in the stock market?**
- **Are you familiar with your own company stock?**
- **Which industry are you the most knowledgeable about?**
- **Have you started to save for your long-term needs?**

CHAPTER

Moving Forward
with Head & Heart

*"If you do not live the life you believe,
you will believe the life you live."*

ZIG ZIGLAR, Motivational Speaker/Writer

Before I send you, my dear readers, off into the world to use the information in this book using both head (active masculine) and heart (passive creative feminine) energies, I want to leave you with a few more thoughts. First, as stated earlier in various ways, "belief" is the most important factor in attaining whatever you want. Remember this. As Ziglar's quote indicates, your belief system is reflected in your life.

Also, for women, I remind you once again that you must be careful not to abandon your positive feminine characteristics as you become more skilled at using your masculine energy. One important female quality that will assist you as you apply the lessons contained in *Financial Security for Women* is the ability to cope when life challenges.

In addition, I want to point out one more time that it's not only women who need to learn to balance their feminine and masculine sides—men do too. In 1993, *Forbes* magazine reported that three-quarters of the total suicides in the US were by white males. The desensitization that society fosters on men—not allowing them to explore their feminine energy—causes them much unhappiness. Although most women have learned to cope, men can sometimes be like sturdy oaks, snapping in two when the harsh winds of life blow on them. Just as this book teaches lessons that have been more a part of the male world, it is my hope that over time more men will realize that there is much to be learned from women—and hence acquire the flexibility and durability of an emerging sapling.

The initiative by women to improve their individual lives, thus creating a better world for all, is easily seen today. In their current book, *Trend Tracking: Strategies for Lifelong Success!*, Gerald Celente and Tom Milton predict: ". . . within this decade, the Sixties mentality [Author's Note: one that was concerned with acknowledging women's capabilities, equal rights for people, opposing wars, lifestyle over money, and a healthy environment for humankind] will have taken over, and it will characterize the next century, the Global Age!"

This view is echoed in Tom Harpur's *The Thinking Person's Guide to God*. He says, "I am certain a fresh spiritual awakening is under way as we prepare to enter the third millennium AD, and I am just as certain that women are destined to be in the vanguard." Likewise, Patricia Aburdene and John Nesbitt in *Megatrends for Women* write: ". . . the women of the 1990s are challenging and overturning the male-dominated status quo, reintegrating female values and perspectives, and recasting the social, political and economic megatrends of the day."

Enhancing the Gifts from This Book

Hopefully I have achieved my goals for this book and you have received its gifts—you have been uplifted, you have been inspired to go after the things that you want out of life, and you are moving toward greater self-fulfillment and financial freedom. In addition to the improvement in your intuitive side, you are now willing to do the work necessary to promote your practical side by absorbing and using the investment principles presented.

Now that you have read through the book once, go back with spaced reviews to particular sections until you "own" the material. As stated earlier, even if you have not concerned yourself before with the technical side of finances or have tended to "hate" such things, your desire to explore this now will allow you to take control of your financial well-being. Even if you do at some point hire someone to assist you, it is wise to have a general knowledge of the basic principles of investing.

I have tried to share my knowledge and experiences with you in order that you may succeed in whatever you choose. However knowledge and learning by example are only useful if you are open to receive, and wisdom cannot be taught. It is acquired through a "do-it-yourself" process. It comes from living life to the fullest.

Go with God

Do you recall the Jedi master's admonition to Luke Skywalker in the movie *Star Wars:* "The Force be with you"? You can tap into this Force in your own life by listening to your heart. This Higher Self within is your Power. It does not matter if you call it God, Jesus Christ, Chi, Prana, Buddha, Higher Power, the Force, the Universe, etc. If I were talking with Luke, I would probably say, "Go with God," or as the Spanish say, "Vaya con Dios." This divine grace is called forth in the beautiful poem dedicated to me by my life-long friend, Mary Jane Barrett Butler, at the time of my first wedding. Mary Jane was my matron of honor. The verse was written on the inside of the missal that she gave me to carry at the ceremony.

To Mitzi (my nickname) from Mary Jane 8/20/52:

> *Dear friend of mine,*
> *There is no way*
> *In which I could address you*
> *With more sincerity of heart*
> *Than just to say God bless you*
> *My words could wish that all your cares*
> *Would be a little lighter*
> *And I could send you greeting cards*
> *To make your hours brighter*
> *My lips could call good luck to you*
> *Or whisper happy endings*
> *And I could promise you the depth of faithful understanding*
> *But I am sure no other thought*
> *Or message would impress you*
> *As lovingly or lastingly*
> *As asking God to bless you*
> *And so I say God bless you friend*
> *In every good endeavor*
> *And may His guiding grace be yours*
> *Forever and forever.*

202

(We think that James Metcalf wrote the above poem; however, we have not been able to determine what newspaper it appeared in.)

Mary Jane, your beautiful wishes have been fulfilled over and over again. I attribute my success to God's blessings and especially to his grace. Thank you, God, for placing Mary Jane on my Path.

If you have found value in reading this book, please tell others about it—the women as well as the men in your life. Everyone can benefit in some way from reading this book.

Know that you have been given all that you need to become successful with your finances and in every area of your life. And remember that to accomplish this, you must commit to trusting, to giving up fear, and to replacing it with faith (trust).

Finally, in order to convince your Self further that you now possess everything that you need to achieve whatever your Mind can conceive, try incorporating one more practice into your daily life. As often as possible, while looking in a mirror, repeat the phrase, *"I have everything I want or need to be a success right NOW."*

You can do it!

Appendix

GLOSSARY

10-K: Required form filed with the SEC each year wherein the corporation must make details public about the company, its officers and the way it conducts its business.

12 b-1 fees: The government has allowed investment management firms to deduct these costs from the investor's return. While these are legitimate fees that a mutual fund company can use to offset some of its operating costs, they often reduce the return to the investor. It is wise to check into the 12 b-1 fees before purchasing a mutual fund. They can run from as little as .25% to over 2.00% per year.

401(k) plan: A type of qualified plan where the employee contributes most of the money. However, the employer can choose to match the employee's contribution, usually up to a certain percentage. The match may be in any amount. Often the employer offers $.50 for each dollar contributed by the employee up to 6%.

ADR: A certificate for a foreign stock available for purchase on the American stock exchanges. This makes it much easier to participate in the global economy.

Alpha: The alpha is a measurement of how close the return on the investment matched its beta. If the alpha is a positive number, it indicates that the investment did better than expected. This ratio is used in mutual funds. Morningstar has rated most of the mutual funds. It gives the Alpha and the Beta. However it is wise to understand that Morningstar's ratings are for past performance. Often their A-rated funds become D funds the following year. See "Beta."

Alternative Minimum Tax (AMT): See "AMT."

American Stock Exchange (AMEX): This stock exchange trades mostly stocks and bonds of small to medium-sized companies. It is located in New York.

AMEX (American Stock Exchange): See "American Stock Exchange."

AMT (Alternative Minimum Tax): By law, all US citizens must figure the amount of tax that they owe the government with both the regular and the AMT method. See "Preference items."

Annuity: An insurance contract. See "Immediate annuity" and "Deferred annuity."

Appreciation: An increase in the value of a stock, a bond, real estate or other investment.

206

Asset: Something of commercial exchange value owned by an individual or a business. In this book, we consider stocks, bonds, real estate, cash equivalents and cash as assets.

Asset allocation: A strategy for balancing risk within a portfolio by including different classes of assets. For example, including stocks and bonds.

Asset class: The main categories of assets are those mentioned in the definition for "asset."

Back-end load: A load is a commission charged on the purchase of mutual fund shares sold by brokers or other members of a sales force. In an effort to compete with the "no-load" funds, load companies introduced the back-end load concept. Here, the company charges a percentage if the investor sells the shares before the end of the deferred sales charge period (usually six years).

However, on the back-end load funds, the investor receives less return than if the shares were purchased with a front-end load. The reason is that the mutual fund company deducts for the interest it must pay on borrowing the money to compensate the salesperson. When all shares are free of load, they automatically become equal in value to the "front-end load" shares. Also, note that investments held for more than five years (an approach which is highly recommended) are a better value if purchased with a front-end load.

Balanced fund: A mutual fund that invests in stocks, bonds and cash equivalents. See "Mutual fund" and "Cash equivalent."

Balanced portfolio: A portfolio containing several different types of investments. Usually refers to a portfolio that has both stocks and bonds.

Balance sheet: The financial statement that shows what individuals or businesses have in assets as well as liabilities (debt).

BARRA: An internationally recognized technology firm based in Berkeley, California. It constructs several equity indices, including individual ones for large growth stocks, large value stocks, mid-cap 400 growth stocks, mid-cap 400 value stocks and the Sharpe/BARRA small-cap index.

Bear market: A period during which stock prices are generally falling. Quite often when stocks go down, the value of bonds goes up. However this has not proven true in the markets for the 1990s.

Beta: A number that measures the volatility of an investment. Usually a low Beta indicates a less risky investment. The standard is set at 1. For example, 1.5 Beta means that the investment is .5 more volatile than the average investment (based on the Standard & Poor's 500). For mutual funds, the Beta and Alpha are usually listed on the information sheet. Although choosing some mutual funds with low Betas might be all right, including mutual funds with high Betas is prudent, too. See "Alpha."

Bond: A debt security issued by a company, municipality or government agency. The purchaser of a bond is lending money to the issuer. In exchange, the issuer promises to repay the amount of the loan on a specified maturity date. The issuer is also obligated to pay the bondholder periodic fixed-interest payments over the life of the loan.

Book value: A method of measuring a company's worth. It includes the value of the company's real estate, machinery and inventory. It does not include the intangible assets, such as good will, name recognition, etc.

Broker: A person who is registered with the stock exchange in which she/he trades and acts as an intermediary between the buyer and the seller of stocks, bonds and commodities. See "Broker/dealer."

Broker/dealer: An individual who acts as both a broker and a dealer.

Bull market: A period during which stock prices are generally rising. The price of bonds often goes down in a bull market. However, in the 1990s, this has not happened.

Buyout: Normally this term is used when one corporation purchases the assets of another corporation. When this happens, it can be a plus for an investor. The purchaser may offer cash, some of its stock, or both in exchange for the old company's shares.

Capital: A long-term asset that may include security investments or property and equipment. See "Security."

Capital appreciation: The increase in the price of an investment, also known as "growth."

Capital gain or loss: The profit or loss that results from a change in the price of an asset. It is only a "realized" gain or loss if the asset is sold.

Capital gain distribution: The payments to mutual fund shareholders of profits (long-term gains) realized on the sale of the fund's portfolio securities. These amounts are usually paid once a year. The maximum capital gains tax is 20%.

Capitalization: When this term is used for the company's stock, it means the value of all of the stock. Multiplying the share price by the number of outstanding shares derives the number. See "Outstanding shares."

Capital markets: This name encompasses all of the securities markets where individuals can purchase financial investments.

Capital preservation: A method of protecting the value of one's assets.

Cash equivalent: A type of investment that is easily converted into cash. Otherwise known as "dollar denominated." Examples: Money market, savings and checking accounts and CDs.

Cash flow statement: A financial statement of inflows and outflows of cash for individuals. Known as the Profit and Loss Statement (P&L) for a corporation. Monthly statements are helpful; annual ones are a must.

CD (Certificate of Deposit): A negotiable certificate that evidences a time deposit of funds with a bank and is typically backed by the Federal Deposit Insurance Corporation (FDIC) to a maximum of $100,000 per person at any single institution. Always confirm that the FDIC insures a CD in which you invest.

Closed-end mutual fund: The amount of shares in this type of mutual fund is limited. The price of the shares is based on whatever an investor is willing to pay. If it is lower than the net asset value (NAV)—the total market value of the stocks divided by the number of shares—it is selling at a "discount." If higher than the NAV, it is selling at a "premium." When the amount of shares specified is sold out, a buyer must wait until there is a seller.

Collateral: An investor guarantees repayment of a loan or other obligation by putting up property or securities as collateral. Banks and brokerage firms are willing to loan money at discounted rate—lower than regular rates—if there is collateral. See "Margin account."

Commercial loan: A loan issued by a bank institution to a business. See "Consumer loan."

Common stock: An investment instrument that represents ownership in a public corporation. The common stock shareholder votes on certain matters and receives dividends. In the case of liquidation, the bondholders and preferred stockholders get paid first. If there is any money after the company's creditors get paid, the common stockholder is compensated.

Compounding: Interest compounds. This means that it is earned on both the principal and the accumulated interest, and thus the investment return increases dramatically.

Consumer loan: A loan issued by a bank institution to an individual usually at a set rate of interest and with a scheduled payback period. Consumer loans typically are issued for car purchases, home improvements or other personal expenses.

Consumer Price Index (CPI): See "CPI."

Contrarian: A person who buys on bad news and sells on good news. She/he does the opposite of what everyone else is doing, often buying out-of-favor stocks.

Corporate bond: A bond issued by a private corporation. Corporate bonds are usually taxable. Compare to government and municipal bonds.

Cost basis: In most situations, the basis of property is its cost to the taxpayer.

CPI (Consumer Price Index): A measure of inflation or deflation based on price changes in consumer goods and services.

Credit risk: Involves the safety of one's investment. The term is generally associated with bonds, and the risk is that the issuer will default in the payments of either principal or interest, or both. This term can also describe an individual. A good credit risk is an individual who pays her/his bills on time.

Currency: Paper and coins issued by a country. Examples: US dollar, British pound, French franc and Japanese yen.

Current income: This is cash interest or dividends regularly received from investments in bonds or stocks.

Dealer: A dealer is a buyer and seller of financial instruments. She/he also can sell directly to others, as a broker-dealer. However, most often she/he hires a broker as an agent to act in her/his behalf. See "Broker" and "Broker/dealer."

Debt: An obligation of an individual or a company to pay back the money borrowed.

Deferred annuity: A type of annuity that continues to grow tax-deferred. It need never become an immediate annuity. If distributions are taken before age 59½, the annuitant is penalized 10%. All distributions are taxed and are considered gains until the annuitant's cost basis is reached. Then distributions are tax-free. See "Immediate annuity."

Depreciation: The decrease in value of a fixed asset due to a decline in the price and/or wear and tear. Also, the decrease allowed by the IRS in computing the value of property for tax purposes. Also, the decrease in purchasing power or exchange power of currency.

Discounted dollars: An after-tax dollar does not represent a full dollar because it has been reduced by taxes. It could be discounted by as much as 40 cents (39.6% tax bracket). It then would become a 60-cent dollar.

Discount rate: The interest rate charged to member banks that borrow from the Federal Reserve banks.

Diversification: The policy of all mutual funds to spread investments among a number of different securities to reduce the risks inherent in investing. See "Asset allocation."

Dividend Reinvestment Program (DRP): See "DRP."

Dividends: A distribution of earnings of a corporation. The most common form of dividend payment is cash. Note that a company that regularly splits their stock and gives "stock dividends" is a very attractive investment.

Dividend yield: A percentage based on dividing the current market price by the amount of the dividend. For instance, if the market price is much higher than what you paid for the stock, you are receiving a greater dividend yield. Example: The financial section gives the dividend yield at 2%. The market price of the stock is $25. You paid $12.50. You are receiving twice the dividend or 4%.

Dollar-cost averaging: The practice of investing equal amounts of money at regular intervals regardless of whether securities markets are moving up or down. This procedure reduces average share costs to the investor, who acquires more shares in periods of lower securities prices and fewer shares in periods of higher prices.

Domestic fund: A mutual fund containing US stocks, bonds or cash equivalents.

Double-taxed dollars: A term used to describe investment returns that are taxed twice. For example, returns on deferred annuities above cost basis and interest and dividends taxed as corporate profits and again as individual investment income.

Dow Jones Industrial Average (the "DOW"): Tracks 30 large-company stocks traded on the NYSE. The most widely used market indicator, it is composed of 30 large, actively traded stocks.

DRP (Dividend Reinvestment Program): A term used to describe a program wherein stockowners can purchase more shares of the company's stock with their quarterly dividend and/or additional money. This is a painless way to accumulate shares using dollar-cost averaging.

EAFE Index: Ranks the stocks in Europe, Australia and the Far East, specifically Sweden, Switzerland, Australia, United Kingdom, France, Germany, Italy, Netherlands, Japan and other countries—non-specified.

Employee Stock Ownership (ESOP): See "ESOP."

EPS (Earnings Per Share): This represents the number obtained by dividing the net profit for a company by the number of shares.

Equity: The ownership interest of common and preferred stockholders in a corporation.

ESOP: An Employee Stock Ownership Program encourages workers to buy their employer's stock, usually at a reduced price.

Ex-dividend: When the settlement date for a stock or a stock mutual fund occurs after the date for dividend distribution, the new stockholder is not entitled to the dividend.

Expected return: The percentage that an investor expects to receive on an investment. Often the real return and the expected return do not match because the investor's expectations are too high.

FDIC (Federal Deposit Insurance Corporation): A US agency established in 1933, the FDIC guarantees (within limits) funds deposited in the FDIC member banks and thrift institutions. The FDIC also makes loans and buys assets in an effort to prevent bank failures and facilitate mergers.

Financial objective: A calculation based on the amount of money needed, the time period, the expected inflation rate and the expected rate of return. To reach one's financial objective, it is wise to write your financial objective down.

Fixed-income investment: A security such as a bond or a preferred stock. Although the price of the underlying investment can fluctuate, the yield (fixed-income) is always the same.

Front-end load fund: The investor pays a one-time commission to the sales-person. If an investor intends to hold the investment for more than five years, she/he is better off paying the load up front. See "Back-end load."

Fundamentals: The elements for evaluating a company. The basic questions include "How strong is the management?" and "What are the company's prospects?" A good way to find out what the company is doing is by ordering their 10-K.

General obligation bonds: A type of municipal bond backed by the full faith credit and taxing power of the issuer for payment of interest and principal.

GIC: Guaranteed interest contract between an insurance company and a corporate savings or pension plan that offers a fixed rate of return on the capital invested over the life of the contract or for a certain period. Not federally insured.

Global fund: A mutual fund that invests in securities markets both inside and outside the US. See "International fund."

Government bond: 5-, 10-, or long-term (30-year) bonds issued by the federal government.

Growth fund: A type of diversified common stock fund that has capital appreciation as its primary goal.

Growth stock: One whose issuer is growing faster than the average company. Often the price reflects the company's growth prospects.

Guaranteed interest contract: Usually offered by an insurance company stating that it will guarantee the investor a definite interest rate. The rate is usually established each year, however it may be a blending of five years of rates, which is called a "rolling average." See "GIC."

Hard asset: Real estate, jewelry, gold, art, etc.

High yield bonds: Sometimes known as "junk bonds," these are issued by companies that have to pay a higher interest rate on their bonds in order to find a buyer for their debt. At times, the reason for this is that it is a "start-up" company or the company already has a lot of debt. The best way to participate in this market is through a mutual fund, which gives you diversification.

Immediate annuity: The contract is turned over to the insurance company for a promise of periodic payments. These can be paid out for the annuitant's life, a period certain or, in a joint annuity, for the life of the surviving spouse at a reduced rate—usually 50%. A company pension is this form of annuity.

Income fund: A type of mutual fund that seeks to provide a stable current income by investing in securities that pay interest or high dividends. Most mutual fund companies include funds with different goals. An example of an income fund is the American Mutual Fund.

Index: For investment purposes, the term "indexed fund" is used to describe a fund that is tied to one of the indexes (Standard & Poor's, Russell 2000, etc.) The fund is not the index; it is made up of the stocks contained in the index, but in a smaller amount. Accordingly, the investor of an indexed fund receives a portion of the dividends paid on the entire index. This is based on the percentage of the fund held.

Index fund: See "Index." Can be based on the Dow Jones, Standard & Poor's (S&P), Wilshire 5000, Russell 2000 or the EAFE. Although this can seem a painless way to invest, exclusively using index funds is not recommended. Also, see article by author in Chapter 13, "Understanding Return on Investment."

Individual Retirement Account (IRA): See "IRA."

Interest rate risk: A risk associated with an investment, which relates to the sensitivity of its price or value to fluctuations in the current level of interest rates. This is usually associated with bond prices, but applies to all investments.

International fund: A mutual fund that invests in securities outside of the US. See "Global fund."

Intrinsic value: A measurement of non-tangible assets, such as goodwill, name recognition and market share.

Investment advisor: Anyone can call herself/himself an investment advisor. However a Registered Investment Advisor (RIA) is an individual who is registered with the Securities Exchange Commission (SEC). Normally this is through the firm's registration.

Investment grade: A corporate or municipal bond that has a rate of AAA (the highest) or BBB (medium-grade) as rated by the Standard & Poor's Corporation. See "Junk bond."

Investment objectives: The investor designs her/his investment portfolio to meet specific needs. It is usually wise to include both income and growth investments. However, if in doubt, invest for growth.

Investment policy statement: This written statement contains the investor's objectives; it also states how much risk the investor is willing to assume.

Investment style: The primary characteristic of the stocks that a fund manager purchases for a mutual fund. The six styles include large growth, large value, mid growth, mid value, small growth and small value.

IRA (Individual Retirement Account): A retirement account, tax-deductible under certain conditions, for self-employed and other employed individuals.

Junk bond: This is a bond rated lower than BBB. See definitions for "Investment-grade" and "High yield bonds." Although it is probably unwise to invest in individual junk bonds, it is usually safe to include a junk bond fund in your portfolio as it contains many such bonds.

Laddering: A method of diversifying bond portfolios by using bonds with different maturities.

Large capitalization (large cap) stock: A stock in a company with a market capitalization of 4.5 billion US dollars or greater.

Large growth stock: A large cap stock which has exhibited greater than average growth over a period.

Large value stock: A large cap stock that seems to be priced lower than its true worth. This may be because of the industry it is in or the individual company may be "out of favor" in the market.

Limited market order: See "Stop order" and "Market order."

Limited partner: The investor in a limited partnership is liable only up to her/his investment. The general partner assumes the largest risk. See "Limited partnership."

Limited partnership: A group of properties or companies put together by a general partner or syndicator who then sells shares in the larger group. Examples of these partnerships are oil and gas, cable and real estate (REITS). See "REITS."

Liquidity: The ability to cash in all or part of your mutual fund shares on any business day and receive their current value (which may be more or less than your original cost).

Load (sales load or charge): A commission charged on the purchase of mutual fund shares sold by brokers or other members of a sales force. The sales charge may not exceed 8.5% of the initial investment. The charge is added to the net asset value per share when determining the offering price. However, depending on the amount of shares bought, the offering price could be less.

Load fund: A mutual fund that is sold through a sales force and not directly by the mutual fund company, which sells mostly "no-load" funds. Please note the word "mostly." Some mutual fund companies who sell directly to the public sell both "no-load" and load funds. Make certain that you know what you are buying.

Years ago, the load percentage was commonly at 8.5%. Currently, because of the increased competition from the mutual fund companies who sell direct, loads are usually below 5.75%. This may seem high, however if the fund has a superior record of accomplishment, this percentage spread over the necessary five-year holding period is negligible.

Long-term: An investment held over five years.

Margin accounts: This account is set up by the brokerage firm to allow the investor to borrow 50-60% (brokerage houses differ in the amount they will loan) against the value of the securities in her/his account. The interest rates charged are quite competitive—usually lower than bank loans—and all margin interest is tax deductible if the proceeds are used for investing. See "Collateral."

Marginal tax bracket: The rate at which a person is taxed on additional dollars over the bulk of her/his income. This income could be from bonuses or part-time employment. One can lower her/his marginal tax bracket in several ways. For instance, by placing $2,000 in a tax-deductible IRA, you might lower your income enough to reduce your marginal tax rate. Or you might shift some income into the following year. Also, remember that the taxpayer has the choice of claiming tax-deductible expenses in either the year that they are incurred or in the year paid.

Market capitalization: See "Capitalization."

Market order: An order to buy/sell a stock at the market price. See "Stop order."

Market risk: In general, the risk based on the variations in the price of market securities. Specifically, this is the risk over time that the whole market, asset class, or sub-class will suffer a down period.

Market timing: The attempt to sell investments at their highest price and to buy them at their lowest price. Market-timers are not successful investors.

Maturity: The date on which the principal amount of the note, bond or other debt security becomes due and payable.

Medium capitalization (mid-cap) stock: A stock whose market capitalization is between 1 billion and 4.5 billion US dollars.

Mid-cap growth stock: A stock whose capitalization is between 1 billion and 4.5 billion and whose company strives to please its shareholders through growing internally, either not paying dividends or paying low dividends.

Mid-cap value stock: A stock whose capitalization is between 1 billion and 4.5 billion and whose company strives to please its shareholders by offering them a more stable stock price and dividends.

Monetary policy: The policies and actions of the Federal Reserve Board that affect the rate of growth and size of the money supply.

Money market fund: An investment company that invests in money market instruments with maturities of less than one year. Usually these funds are sold no-load and offer draft-writing privileges.

Municipal bond: A debt security issued by a state or a municipality, such as a city or county, to raise money to finance its capital expenditures.

Mutual fund: Mutual fund shares are redeemable immediately at the NAV (Net Asset Value) of the shares. Usually this can be accomplished by telephone and a check is sent out immediately; or the redemption funds can be wired directly into the investor's bank account. Also, many of the mutual fund companies, which charge a load, waive the load if the investor repurchases the shares within 60 days. See "NAV," "Closed-end mutual fund," and "Open-end mutual fund."

NASD (National Association of Securities Dealers, Inc.): A self-regulated organization for member securities-brokerage firms. The NASD has authority over the distribution of mutual fund shares.

NASDAQ: An automated quotation system owned by the NASD. This computerized system provides brokers and dealers with price quotations for securities not traded in the large stock exchanges.

National Association of Securities Dealers, Inc. (NASD): See "NASD."

NAV (Net Asset Value): The market worth of one share of a mutual fund. This figure is derived by taking a fund's total assets—securities, cash and any accrued earnings—deducting liabilities, and dividing by the number of shares outstanding.

Net worth: Assets minus liabilities. For an individual, net worth is the value of all possessions, including property and securities, minus debts, including mortgages.

New York Stock Exchange (NYSE): A corporation operated by a board of directors responsible for setting policy, supervising the exchange and member activities, listing securities, and overseeing the transfer of members/ seats on the exchange. The NYSE is the most active stock exchange, and it trades primarily shares in well-established companies.

No-load mutual fund: A mutual fund selling its shares at net asset value without any front or back-end sales charge.

Non US: International mutual funds that do not include any US stocks.

NYSE (New York Stock Exchange): See "New York Stock Exchange."

Offering price: The price an investor will pay, per share, to enter a mutual fund.

Open-end mutual fund: A limitless number of shares that are priced at NAV and offering price. See "NAV" and "Offering price."

Outstanding shares: At times, a company has issued a certain number of shares—sometimes to fulfill future employee-stock options. Only the shares that have been sold or are already owned by the employees after exercising their options are called "outstanding" shares.

Partial dollars: See "Discounted dollars."

Par value: The stated value of a security printed on its certificate. A bond's par value is the dollar amount on which interest is calculated as well as the amount paid to holders at maturity.

P/B (Price to book): A valuation ratio. A measurement of value determined by dividing the company's stock price per share by the net worth (assets minus liabilities) per share.

P/E (Price to earnings): The price divided by earnings. A measurement of valuation determined by dividing the company's stock price (per share) by its profits per share.

Performance: The growth of the value of an asset. The performance of an asset may be positive or negative, often compared to performance of appropriate market indices or "benchmarks," such as assets in the same asset class, assets in different asset classes, the stock market as a whole, etc.

Portfolio: The combined holdings of more than one stock, bond or cash equivalent by an individual or a company.

Preference items: Items added back into the tax calculations to figure taxes using the Alternative Minimum Tax (AMT) rates of 26%—incomes less than $175,000—and 28%—incomes over $175,000. Examples: Tax-exempt income, exemptions for children, etc. See "AMT."

Preferred stock: An investment instrument that represents ownership of a public corporation. This class of stock offers fixed dividends without voting privileges.

Price to Book (P/B): See "P/B."

Price to Earnings (P/E): See "P/E."

Prime rate: The interest rates that commercial banks charge their prime or most creditworthy customers (generally large corporations).

Principal: The face value of a deposit or debt. In other words, the amount deposited or borrowed on which interest is paid. The principal amount does not include interest earned or accrued.

Prospectus: A legal document that must be given to every investor who purchases registered securities in an offering. It describes the details of the company, the fund, and the particular offering or investment objective, charges and expenses.

Proxy statement: Information that is required by the SEC to inform shareholders about company matters before they vote by proxy on items submitted to shareholders for approval. This statement must include the names of the members of the board, their salaries, and other pertinent information. When a shareholder votes by proxy, they select a representative to vote in their behalf at the company's meetings.

Qualified plan: A tax-deferred retirement plan set up by an employer for benefit of employees. Employees may contribute to the plan, which is regulated by the Internal Revenue Service (IRS). Employees may draw from the plan only at retirement or termination of employment.

Rate of return: Stocks—The percentage of increase/decrease of dividends received plus capital appreciation or the market value of stock shares. Bonds —One measure is yield, the coupon or contractual interest rate, divided by the purchase price. The interest income plus appreciation/depreciation measure the total return on bonds.

Real Estate Investment Trust (REIT): See "REIT."

Real return: The rate of return adjusted for inflation. If your rate of return over 10 years averaged 10% and inflation averaged 4%, your real return was 6%.

Redeem: Selling shares back to the mutual fund. Mutual fund shares are redeemable on any business day.

Redemption fee: A fee paid by the bond issuer if it "calls" or cancels the bond contract before maturity. Also, the fee paid by the issuer of preferred stock if it terminates the contract before maturity. Also, the fee paid on distributions from "back-ended" mutual funds before the penalty period is over. Also, the fee paid should an annuity owner cash in the annuity before the penalty period is over.

Reinvestment risk: The risk of not being able to invest the proceeds from a fixed-income investment at the same or better return.

REIT (Real Estate Investment Trust): A group of real estate holdings managed by a general partner for its shareholders (limited partners). REITs are invested in a diversified portfolio of various types of real estate, including shopping centers, hotels and apartment complexes.

Return: Profit or loss on an investment, usually expressed as a percentage.

Revenue bond: A bond whose interest and principal are payable only from specific earnings of an income-producing enterprise.

Risk: The possibility that the actual return on an investment might be lower than expected. Usually the more risk that is assumed, the greater the return.

Risk-adjusted return: The term "risk-free rate" is used to compare investments. It is presumed to be the same as the return on 91-day T-bills (90-day T-bills that have matured) plus the risk premium in case of interest-rate fluctuations. The word "presumed" is used because as pointed out in the book, there is no "risk-free" investment.

Risk-free investment: A US Treasury bill is considered a "risk-free" investment. However, the market dictates the price that another investor is willing to pay should you choose or need to sell your Treasury bill before its maturity date. You might not receive all of your money back. There is no such thing as a "risk-free" investment.

Risk-free rate: See "Risk-adjusted return" and "T-bill (Treasury bills)."

Risk premium: The increased return demanded by investors for increased risks experienced with the investments.

Rollover: In an IRA, there are unlimited transfers or rollovers from one fiduciary (the firm holding the retirement assets) to another. However, a distribution can only be taken once a year. If the distribution is returned within 60 days, it is not taxed. If not, it is taxed in the year the distribution was received.

Funds from one employer qualified retirement account to another must always be in the form of a rollover. Any time a distribution is taken from a qualified retirement plan—not an IRA—the amount is immediately taxed 20%.

Roth IRA: For the tax year starting in 1998, you can put $2,000 post-taxed dollars into an investment termed a Roth IRA. This investment will grow tax-deferred and funds are not taxed at time of distribution in an investment over five years old.

Russell 2000 Index: Tracks 2000 stocks that are traded on the Over The Counter (OTC) Exchange.

S&P 500 (Standard & Poor's): An index made up of 500 stocks traded on the New York Stock Exchange (NYSE).

Sales charge: See "Load."

SEC (Securities and Exchange Commission): The primary US federal agency that regulates registration and distribution of mutual fund shares.

Sector fund: See "Specialized fund."

Security: A financial asset that is not a "hard" asset. This would include stock and bond certificates, options, warrants, etc. See "hard asset" and "warrant."

SIPC (Securities Investor Protection Corporation): A non-profit corporation established in the US to protect the investor. All broker/dealers registered with the SEC and national exchanges must be members of the SIPC.

The SIPC insures securities to $500,000 and cash to $100,000. This insures against the failure of the brokerage firm, not against market loss.

Small-cap growth fund: A fund that is made up of small-capitalization stocks. The fund manager's focus is on growth, not on dividends or income.

Small-capitalization stock (small-cap): The stock of relatively small firms with little equity and few shares outstanding. Because the stock is "thinly traded"—i.e., it does not have many shares outstanding—the price tends to go up and down more than large-cap stocks. Market value is under 1 billion US dollars.

Small-cap value fund: A fund that is made up of small-capitalization stocks. The fund manager is interested in stability of companies and dividends.

Specialized fund: A type of mutual fund that tries to achieve its investment objectives by concentrating its investments within a single industry or group of related industries. Also called a "sector fund."

Spousal IRA: If one of the spouses is not working, the working spouse can deduct a Spousal IRA of $2,250. This amount can be divided so that the non-working spouse receives the $2,000 IRA and the other spouse receives the $250 spousal IRA.

Spread: The difference between the bid and asked price of a security.

Standard & Poor's (S&P 500): See "S&P 500."

Stock: Either a common or preferred stock is a partial ownership in a company.

Stock dividends: Often companies focused on growth offer their stockholders dividends in the form of stock splits. See "Stock split."

Stock options: These are options to buy a company's stock at a particular price. They are offered to employees as incentives in place of or in addition to good salaries. If the price of the stock rises, the employee may cash in her/his options and either keep the stock in her/his portfolio, or sell the stock.

Stock split: The division of a corporation's sold shares into a greater/lesser number. Normally this is an increase in shares. The multiple might be two for one, wherein the investor receives one additional share for each share that she/he holds. See "Stock dividends."

Stop order: An individual wishing to buy or sell a stock can place a stop order on the transaction. In other words, she/he stops any buying or selling that is not at the price that she/he has set. This method of investing can offer some security as the investor can force a sale of a stock whose price is falling. See "Market order."

Style: See "investment style."

Sub-asset class: An asset class that falls under one of the three main asset classes—equity, fixed income and cash/cash equivalents. Example: A small cap growth stock is a sub-asset class of a type of equity.

T-Bill (Treasury bill): A marketable, short-term (90-day to 1-year) US government debt security issued through competitive bidding process at discount from face value. T-Bills are backed by the full faith and credit of the US government.

Thinly traded stock: See "Small capitalization stock."

Total return: A measure of an investment's performance that takes into account all three components of earnings per share: dividends, capital gain distributions and price appreciation.

Treasury bill (T-Bill): See "T-Bill."

Valuation: Assigning a price or worth to a company's assets or its stock. Several methods are commonly used, such as book value, liquidation value and intrinsic value. The company's amount of debt, its bad debts and/or its depreciation influence the valuation.

Variable annuity: An annuity invested in mutual funds—mostly stocks and bonds—sold inside an insurance "wrapper." See "Fixed annuity."

Volatility: The tendency to experience fluctuations in price of a stock.

Warrant: A right given to an investor to purchase a stock or a bond in the company at a certain price. Normally the stock or bond price has to go higher in order for the investor to exercise the warrant. Warrants have a dollar value, however the value is based on the possibility of the warrant becoming more valuable.

Wilshire 5000: An index of over 7000 (originally 5000) small, medium and large companies.

Yield: The income per share paid to a shareholder over a specific time period. Yield is expressed as a percent of the fund's current price per share. For example, if your fund distributed $1.00 per share over a year and, at the end of the year, its price was $20, its yield would be 5%. $1÷$20 = 5%.

Yield–to-maturity: The investor must hold the investment to maturity in order to be guaranteed that she/he will receive back the original investment.

Zero coupon bond: A bond that pays no current interest but is sold at a deep discount from face value. However taxes must be paid each year on appreciation. Example, an EE savings bond.

RESOURCES

Information

These following places are sources of publications that will assist you in doing your own research or in supplementing your broker's information:

Financial Information Services
60 Madison Avenue, 6th Floor
New York, NY 10010
1-800-342-5647 / 1-212-413-7601

> Formerly Moody's. Financial Information Services publishes eight manuals annually giving financial and operating data, company histories, product descriptions, plant and property locations, and lists of company officers. Also, Moody's handbooks are soft-covered, quarterly, and give overviews of 2,200 corporations. Moody's also gives bond ratings. Expensive: Best read in the library.

Standard & Poor's
25 Broadway
New York, NY 10004
1-800-221-5277 / 1-212-208-3965

> Provides financial information as well as ratings on stocks, bonds and insurance. Also an expensive source.

Value Line
711 Third Avenue
New York, NY 10017
1-800-634-3583 / 1-212-687-3965

> Publishes *Value Line Investment Survey* as well as *The Value Line OTC Special Situations Service, Value Line Options,* and *Value Line Convertibles.* Again, the library is best source.

American Association of Individual Investors
625 North Michigan Avenue
Chicago, IL 60611-3110
1-800-322-4237 / 1-312-280-0170

> This association was founded as a nonprofit organization in 1978. Its mission statement is: "To assist individuals to become effective managers of their own assets." The group provides a wealth of information on investing and I highly recommend membership. Their *Inquiry Package* is available at no cost.

Financial Planners

Council of Better Business Bureaus, Inc.
Publication Department
4200 Wilson Boulevard, 8th Floor
Arlington, VA 22203

 Provides *Tips on Financial Planners.* Cost: $1.00 plus SASE with $.87 postage.

International Association for Financial Planning
2 Concourse Parkway
Atlanta, GA 30328

 Provides *Consumer's Guide to Financial Independence*—a workbook to get you started. Cost: $1.00

Institute of Certified Financial Planners
3801 East Florida Avenue, Suite 708
Denver, CO 80210-2544
1-800-322-4237

 Membership organization for Certified Financial Planners. Provides a list titled *Selecting a Qualified Financial Planning Professional.* No cost.

Investment Clubs

National Association of Investors Corp. (NAIC)
711 W. Thirteen Mile Rd.
Madison Heights, MI 48071
1-248-583-6242; fax 1-248-883-4880

 Sponsors investment clubs throughout the nation.

BIBLIOGRAPHY

AUTHOR'S NOTE:

All writings brought to our attention are meant to teach us something. Keeping an open mind and being ready and willing to receive information is necessary for growth.

Throughout my life I have included at least 15 to 20 minutes of uplifting reading in my daily schedule, including not only inspirational works but also autobiographies and biographies. Intuitively, I knew that my serious reading had to be balanced by other reading just for enjoyment, but reading non-inspirational things seemed like escapism. Now I understand that all experiencing needs balance. I have learned to truly enjoy—and not feel guilty about—reading mysteries, novels and even science fiction.

My son Bill introduced me to the writings of Dean Koontz, a skilled author whose books always keep my interest. Although they would never be classified as inspirational, I usually find something meaningful in them. I wanted to use a quotation from Koontz's *The Hideaway*—a statement made by his heroine, a young girl of perhaps 12: (paraphrased) "I was always taught that if there is no discussion between two people, one of them is not needed." I felt it would support my belief that disagreements between people are not bad, but are vital.

Unfortunately, I couldn't locate the quotation; but while trying to uncover it, I read another of Koontz's books, *Lightening,* a story based on time travel. In the final chapter, Koontz's heroine, a woman who seemingly has had a miserable life, says something like, "As a child I learned to endure; as an adult, after Danny was killed, I learned to fight. I still endure and I still fight; however, now I have learned that Fate *is.*"

Indeed, this is the message contained in *Financial Security for Women: Using Your Head AND Your Heart to Achieve It.* At times, it is correct to be passive—to endure; at other times, we must fight—take action; but above all, we must understand that there is a Force governing everything. Listen for direction, act, and then accept "Fate." Allow your heart to lead you to the books that will help you to grow. Here are some that have helped me:

Psychology/Spirituality

* Aberdene, Patricia and Naisbitt, John, *Megatrends for Women,* Villard Books—Random House, 1992.

Ban Breathnach, Sarah, *Simple Abundance—A Daybook of Comfort and Joy,* Warner Books, Inc., New York, NY, 1995.

* Barker, Dr. Raymond Charles, *Money Is God in Action,* Devorss & Company, Marina del Rey, CA, 1989 (24th printing).

* Beebe-Hill, Ruth, *Hanta Yo,* Doubleday & Company, Garden City, NY, 1979.

Buchman, Ph.D., Dian Dincin, *The Complete Book of Water Therapy*, Keats Publishing, Inc. New Canaan, CT, 1994.

Chopra, M.D., Deepak, *Seven Spiritual Laws of Success*, Amber-Allen Publishers, 1995. (cassette available)

Choquette, Sonia, *Your Heart's Desire—Instructions for Creating the Life You Really Want*, Crown Publishing, Three Rivers Press, 1997.

* Cole-Whittaker, Terry, *Love and Power in a World Without Limits*, Harper Paperbacks (Division of Harper & Row Publishers), New York, NY, 1989.

Dyer, Ph.D., Wayne W., *Real Magic—Creating Miracles in Everyday Life*, Harper Paperbacks (Division of Harper Collins Publishers), New York, NY, 1992.

Emerson, Ralph Waldo, *Essays*, Harper Collins, New York, NY, 1976.

Gibran, Kahlil, *The Treasured Writings of Kahlil Gibran*, Castle (Div. of Book Sales, Inc.), Secaucus, NJ, 1995.

* Hesse, Herman, *Sidhartha*, New Directions Publishing House, New York, NY, 1951 (43rd printing).

Hill, Napoleon, *Think & Grow Rich*, Ballantine Books, New York, NY, 1976. (also in Spanish and cassette available)

Holzer, Ph.D., Hans, *The Healing Powers of Zeev Kolman—The Secret of Healing—True Story*, Beyond Words Publishing, Inc., Hillsboro, Oregon, 1995.

James, William, *The Varieties of Religious Experience—A Study in Human Nature*, MacMillan Publishing Company, New York, NY, 1997.

* Johnson, Tom, *You Are Always Your Own Experience*, Los Arboles Publications, Redondo Beach, CA, 1989.

* Leboeuf, Ph.D., Michael, *Imagineering—How to Profit From Your Creative Powers*, Berkley Books (previously by McGraw-Hill Book Co.), New York, NY, 1986. (cassette still available)

Leboeuf, Ph.D., Michael, *Working Smart—How to Accomplish More in Half the Time*, Warner Books, New York, NY, 1993.

Mahesh Yogi, Maharishi, *Science of Being and Art of Living—Transcendental Meditation (Revised)*, Maharishi Vedic, Meridian Books, Asbury Park, NJ, 1994.

Morrissey, Mary Manin, *Building Your Field of Dreams*, Bantam Books, NY 1997. (cassette available)

Muktananda, Swami, *Where Are You Going?—A Guide to the Spiritual Journey*, SYDA Foundation, South Fallsburg, NY, 1987. (Many other titles are available from this author.)

Murphy, Dr. Joseph, *The Power of Your Subconscious Mind,* Prentice-Hall, Inc., Englewood Cliffs, NJ, 1988.

Ponder, Catherine, *The Dynamic Laws of Prosperity,* Devorss & Company, Marina del Rey, CA, 1988.

Redfield, James, *The Celestine Prophecy,* Warner Books, New York, NY, 1997.

Siebert, Ph.D., Al, *The Survivor Personality,* A Perigee Book, The Berkley Publishing Group, New York, NY, 1996.

Siegel, M.D., Bernie S., *Love, Medicine & Miracles—Lessons Learned About Self-Healing From a Surgeon's Experience With Exceptional Patients,* Harper & Row Publishers, New York, NY, 1990.

* Silva, Jose and Goldman, Burt, *The Silva Mind Control Method of Mental Dynamics—You Can Unleash the Power of Your Mind to Solve Any Problem,* Pocket Books (Div. of Simon & Schuster), New York, NY, 1988. (Cassette available).

Zi, Nancy, *The Art of Breathing—Six Simple Lessons to Improve Performance, Health and Well-Being,* Vivi Publishing, Glendale, CA, 1996. (cassette available)

Investing

Allen, Robert C., *Creating Wealth,* Simon & Schuster, New York, NY, 1986.

* Amling, Ph.D., Frederick and Droms, D.B.A., C.F.A., William G., *Personal Financial Management,* Irwin, Hometown, IL, 1982.

Applegarth, Ginger, *The Money Diet,* Viking, New York, NY, 1995.

* Beyer, C.F.P., Esther M. (with Church, Connie), *Money Smart—Secrets Women Need to Know About Money,* Simon & Schuster, New York, NY, 1993.

Briggs, Carol, *The Medicine Woman's Guide to Being in Business For Yourself: How to Live Your Spiritual Vision in a Money-Based World,* Earth Nation Publishing, 1992.

* Clayton, Ph.D., Gary E. and Spivey, Ph.D., Christopher B., *The Time Value of Money,* W. B. Saunders Company, Philadelphia, PA, 1982.

Devine, Jr., William Francis, *Women, Men & Money—The Four Keys for Using Money to Nourish Your Relationship, Bankbook and Soul,* Harmony Books, New York, NY, 1998.

* Diamond, Ann B., *Fear of Finance,* Harper Business (Div. of Harper Collins Publishers), New York, NY, 1994.

Dominguez, Joseph and Robin, Vicki, *Your Money or Your Life,* Viking-Penguin, New York, NY, 1993.

* Dreman, David, *The New Contrarian Investment Strategy,* Random House, New York, NY, 1982. (Other titles are available from this author.)

Dunnan, Nancy, *Dun & Bradstreet—Guide to $Your Investments$ 1999,* Harper Collins Publishers, Inc., New York, NY, 1999.

Hayes, Ph.D., Christopher and Kelly, Kate, *Money Makeovers,* Doubleday, New York, NY, 1998.

Kobliner, Beth, *Personal Finance In Your Twenties and Thirties—Get a Financial Life,* Fireside (Division of Simon & Schuster), New York, NY, 1996. (cassette available)

* Lee, Anita Jones, *Women & Money—A Guide for the 90's,* Barrons Educational Series, Hauppauge, NY, 1991.

Lynch, Peter, *Beating the Street,* Fireside (Division of Simon & Schuster), New York, NY, 1994. (abridged cassette available)

* Mamis, Justin, *The Nature of Risk—Stock Market Survival & The Meaning of Life,* Addison-Wesley Publishing Company, Inc., Reading, MA, 1991.

Mays, June, *Women's Guide to Financial Self-Defense,* Time-Warner, New York, NY, June, 1997.

Michaels, Eileen, *When Are You Entitled to New Underwear and Other Major Financial Decisions—Making Your Money Dreams Come True,* MacMillan, New York, NY, 1997.

Michalko, Michael, *Thinkertoys—A Handbook of Business Creativity for the 90s,* 10 Speed Press, Berkeley, CA, 1991.

* Perritt, Gerald, *Small Stocks BIG Profits,* DOW Jones—Irwin, Homewood, IL, 1988.

* Porter, Sylvia, *New Money Book for the 80s,* Doubleday & Company, New York, NY, 1979.

* Savage, Terry, *New Money Strategies for 90s,* Harper Business, New York, NY, 1995.

Siegel, Jeremy J., *Stocks for the Long Run,* McGraw Hill, New York, NY, 1998.

Sivys, Michael, *Rules of Investing,* Warner Books, New York, NY, 1996.

Wolff, Michael, *Net Money—Guide to Total Financial Success Using the Internet or Online Services,* Wolf Media, LLC, Lankam, MD, 1997.

* The books marked with an asterisk are formally "out of print," however most bookstores offer a search service to locate older books. Among these are Barnes & Noble and Borders—plus a small Chicago-land bookstore, Palos Books Ltd. 1-708-430-5977; fax: 1-708-430-5978.

INDEX

Great Gift Idea!

To order more copies of

Financial Security for Women
Using Your Head and Heart to Achieve It

By mail: Fill out this form and mail to
             Symmetry Publishing Company
             P.O. Box 81950
             Chicago, IL 60681-0950

By fax: Fill out this form and fax to **312-228-0600**

By phone: Call **312-228-0595**. Please have credit card information ready.

Online: Visit **www.symmetrypub.com**

Name _____

Address _____

City/State/Zip _____

Daytime phone (in case of questions) (_____) _____

☐ *Personal financial consulting available. Check here for more information.*

☐ *Corporate/nonprofit workshops available. Check here for more information.*

	Quantity*	Cost	Amount
Financial Security for Women		**$29.95**	
*If ordering 3 or more books, deduct 10%		–	
Subtotal			
Sales Tax (IL residents only)—8.75%		+	
Shipping (Priority Mail)/Handling ($5 for first book; $3 for each additional book)		+	
TOTAL			

I understand that I may return books for a full refund for any reason—no questions asked.

Payment Method (Please do not send cash)

☐ Check or money order payable to **Symmetry Publishing Co.** enclosed

☐ Credit card: __Visa __MasterCard __ American Express

Card # ⎿⏌⏌⏌⏌⎿⏌⏌⏌⏌⎿⏌⏌⏌⏌⎿⏌⏌⏌ Expiration Date ⎿⏌–⎿⏌

Signature _____

Please send me a FREE three-year supply of financial recording forms from

Financial Security for Women
Using Your Head and Heart to Achieve It

You'll receive three each of the following forms:

- Budget: Monthly Expense Forecasting
- Budget: Monthly Income Forecasting
- Annual Balance Sheet
- Annual Cash Flow Statement

Please send forms to:

Name _____

Address _____

City/State/Zip _____

We'd love to know what you liked best about **Financial Security for Women.** *Please write comments below:*

_____

_____

_____

☐ *Personal financial consulting available. Check here for more information.*
☐ *Corporate/nonprofit workshops available. Check here for more information.*

Please copy this form, fill it out and send it to

Symmetry Publishing Company
P.O. Box 81950
Chicago, IL 60681-0950

Great Gift Idea!

To order more copies of

Financial Security for Women
Using Your Head and Heart to Achieve It

By mail: Fill out this form and mail to
Symmetry Publishing Company
P.O. Box 81950
Chicago, IL 60681-0950

By fax: Fill out this form and fax to **312-228-0600**

By phone: Call **312-228-0595**. Please have credit card information ready.

Online: Visit **www.symmetrypub.com**

Name _____

Address _____

City/State/Zip _____

Daytime phone (in case of questions) (_____) _____

☐ *Personal financial consulting available. Check here for more information.*

☐ *Corporate/nonprofit workshops available. Check here for more information.*

	Quantity*	Cost	Amount
Financial Security for Women		**$29.95**	
*If ordering 3 or more books, deduct 10%		–	
Subtotal			
Sales Tax (IL residents only)—8.75%		+	
Shipping (Priority Mail)/Handling ($5 for first book; $3 for each additional book)		+	
TOTAL			

I understand that I may return books for a full refund for any reason—no questions asked.

Payment Method (Please do not send cash)

☐ Check or money order payable to **Symmetry Publishing Co.** enclosed

☐ Credit card: __Visa __MasterCard __ American Express

Card # ⎕⎕⎕⎕ ⎕⎕⎕⎕ ⎕⎕⎕⎕ ⎕⎕⎕⎕ Expiration Date ⎕⎕–⎕⎕

Signature _____